YOUNG STUDENTS

Learning Library®

VOLUME 3

Asia —
Blackfoot

NEWFIELD
PUBLICATIONS
SHELTON, CONNECTICUT

CREDITS

Page 260 Spectrum; 261 Christine Osborne; 264 F.A.O. Photo; 265 Tourist Authority of Thailand; 267 Japan Tourist Office (left); Hutchison Library (bottom); 270 Royal Astronomical Society; 271 NASA; 273 Mansell Collection; 274 ZEFA; 277 Dennis Gibert; 278 Solarfilma (top); British Library (bottom); 280 Science Museum; 283 National Gallery of Art, Washington (middle Right); Geological Institute (bottom); 284 Zefa; 285 Australian News & Information Bureau; 287 Australian News & Information Bureau; 288 Australian News & Information Bureau; 289 ZEFA; 290 Christine Osborne; 292 ZEFA; 293 British Leyland; 296 General Motors Corp.; 297 Ford; 298 Allsport, John Audretti; 299 Vermont Development Dept.; 300 Armando Curcio Editore; 308 Museum für Geschichte der Stadt Leipzig (middle); Armando Curcio Editore (bottom); 309 Mansell Collection; 311 ZEFA; 314 Allied Bakeries Ltd.; 316 Phillips Collection Washington DC; 317 Anthony Crickmay (middle); BBC

(bottom); 319 Imperial War Museum; 320 AGE fotostock; 322 Bank of England; 323 The Bank of England (left); ZEFA (right); 325 Hutchison Library; 327 Bridgeman Art Library (bottom left); Armando Curcio Editore (bottom right); 329 Armando Curcio Editore; 330 Armando Curcio Editore; 331 Allsport; 333 Mark Littell; 336 Duomo; 338 Biofotos; 343 ZEFA; 348 Beethovenhaus, Bonn; 349 NHPA; 350 Armando Curcio Editore (top); Associated Press (bottom); 351 E.E.C.; 353 Armando Curcio Editore (top); Mansell Collection (bottom); 356 ZEFA; 357 United States National Archives; 358 United States National Archives; 360 ZEFA; 361 Trinity College, Dublin; 362 Stefan Morris (left); Cycling Tourist Club (bottom right); 366 ZEFA; 372 NHPA; 373 ZEFA; 376 Panos; 378 ZEFA; Peter Newark; 380 Bettmann Archive; 381 Bettman Archive; 382 Bettman Archive; 383 Frank Spooner/Gamma (top); Allsport (middle); Frank Spooner (bottom); 384 Mansell Collection.

Young Students Learning Library and Newfield Publications are federally registered trademarks of Newfield Publications, Inc.

Printed in the U.S.A.

ISBN 0-8374-9812-0

CONTENTS

▲ Teams of trained lifesavers join in the annual parade of lifesaving clubs in **AUSTRALIA.**

ASIA

Asia is the largest continent. It is larger than North and South America combined and covers almost one-third of the world's land area. More than half of all the people in the world live in Asia, which also has the world's highest mountains, broadest plateaus, and largest plains.

Asia stretches about 6,900 miles (11,100 km) from western Turkey northeastward to northern Siberia. In a north-south direction, the continent extends from far above the Arctic Circle to below the equator—a total distance of 5,300 miles (8,500 km). The major countries of Asia are India, China, Japan, and Russia. Russia is partly in Europe but mostly in Asia. The Arabian peninsula and the Middle East are on the western fringe of Asia. (See the articles on ARABIA and the MIDDLE EAST.)

Land and Climate

The borders of India, Afghanistan, Tajikistan (formerly a republic of the Soviet Union), and China all meet at the Pamir knot, a high place in central Asia called "the roof of the world." From this knot of cold, high, rocky land, huge mountain ranges stretch out in many directions like crooked roots of a tree. The Sulaiman and Hindu Kush mountains run hundreds of miles from the Pamirs into Southwest Asia. The Tien Shan and Kunlun mountains extend northeast and east into China, Mongolia, and Tibet for more than 1,000 miles (1,600 km).

The mightiest mountains of all, the Karakorams and the Himalayas, branch southeast from the Pamirs and cut off the Indian subcontinent from China. Eighty-eight of the ninety highest peaks in the world are found in these two mountain ranges. The tallest is Mount Everest in the Himalayas. It is 29,028 feet (8,848 m) high.

Many of the great rivers of Asia begin in these mountains. On the Indian subcontinent side, the Indus, the Brahmaputra, and the Ganges begin their long routes to the Indian Ocean. North of the Himalayas in the plateau of Tibet, the Mekong River flows southward to Southeast Asia. The Chang Jiang and Huang He rivers flow eastward through China.

Almost every kind of climate can be found somewhere in Asia. Cherrapunji, India, has more than 450 inches (11,430 mm) of rainfall a year. In contrast, less than 2 inches (58 mm) of rainfall each year in the Gobi Desert of China and Mongolia. Temperatures often go up to 120°F (49°C) in northern India during May before the rainy season begins. But Oymyakon, in northern Siberia, had one winter day when the temperature dropped to minus 108°F (–78°C).

In Northern China and the northernmost island of Japan the weather is similar to the United States'

▼ The continent of Asia encompasses many different types of landscapes and climates. This desert village is in Syria, one of the countries in the Middle East.

ASIA

Total population
3,202,900,000 people

Highest point
Mount Everest between Tibet (China) and Nepal 29,028 feet (8,848 m)

Lowest point
Dead Sea between Israel and Jordan, 1,320 feet (402 m) below sea level

Longest river
Chang Jiang (Yangtze) 3,915 miles (6,300 km) long

Largest lake
Caspian Sea 169,381 square miles (438,695 sq. km)

Largest city
Tokyo 11,719,000 people

Area
17,135,370 square miles (44,380,400 sq. km)

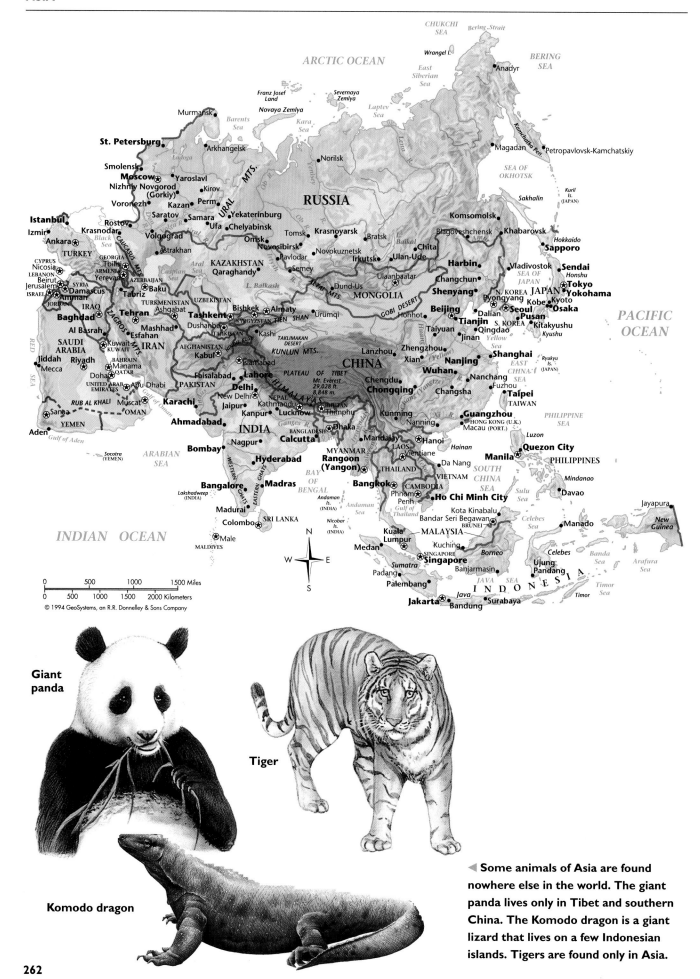

Giant panda

Tiger

Komodo dragon

◀ Some animals of Asia are found nowhere else in the world. The giant panda lives only in Tibet and southern China. The Komodo dragon is a giant lizard that lives on a few Indonesian islands. Tigers are found only in Asia.

Midwest—hot summers and cold winters. Southern Japan, southeastern China, and northern India have a subtropical climate similar to Florida. Winter is dry in India, but in Japan and eastern China rain falls during all four seasons.

Large deserts spread over much of central and southwestern Asia. The mountains surrounding these regions cut off moist air from the sea.

The climate of the Indian subcontinent, Southeast Asia, and China is controlled by powerful winds called *monsoons*. These winds change their direction with the seasons. During the summer, the monsoons blow from the southeast, off the Indian Ocean or along Asia's Pacific coast. They bring drenching rain to India and neighboring countries. Sheets of water attack the land. Sometimes too much rain causes serious flooding and crops are destroyed. During the winter, the monsoons blow from the northeast, off the land, creating a cool, dry season. Dust storms are frequent in parts of China. Not having enough rain destroys crops, too. The lives of

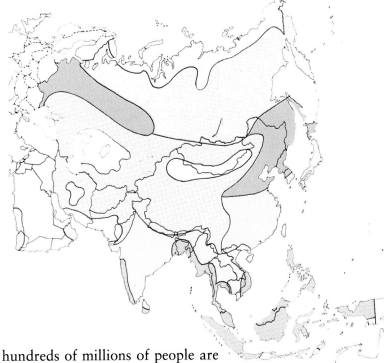

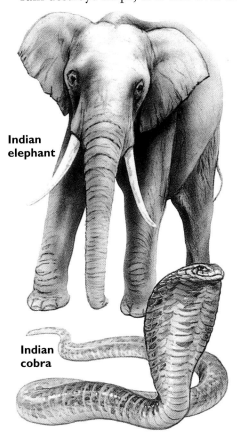

Indian elephant

Indian cobra

hundreds of millions of people are affected by the summer or winter monsoons. Farming is usually done before and after the rainy season.

Animals Large and Small

Thousands of kinds of animals live in Asia, from the mouselike gerbils of the hot deserts to the 10-foot (3-m) Komodo dragon—lizards of rainy Indonesia. Many animals are native only to Asia. Some of these are the Lake Baikal seal of Russia; the snow leopard, found in the Tibetan plateau and China; the Siberian tiger; the orangutan of Borneo and Sumatra; and the giant panda of China.

Tigers, apes, monkeys, elephants, and rhinoceroses live in Southeast Asia. Gazelles live in the hills of dry Southwest Asia. The domesticated camel was once the most important means of transportation in many desert areas of Asia.

Asia is home to a wide range of birds, from the subarctic Siberian murre to the lammergeier, a huge Indian vulture, to the beautiful peacock and lyrebird of Indonesia. Snakes, often poisonous, are plentiful in parts of Asia. Crocodiles and many fish live in southern Asia's rivers and lakes.

CLIMATE REGIONS OF ASIA

☐ **Arctic**
☐ **Subarctic**
☐ **Wet continental**
☐ **Semi-arid**
☐ **Desert**
☐ **Wet subtropical**
☐ **Rainy tropical**
☐ **Wet and dry tropical**

◄ **Two animals from India. The Indian cobra has an extremely poisonous bite.**

263

QUIZ

1. Where is the Gobi desert?
2. Are monsoons wet or windy?
3. Where would you find an orangutan in its native habitat?
4. What is the smallest country (in square miles/sq. km) in Asia?
5. Which country has the fewest people?
6. What religion is practiced in Tibet?
7. To which group of people—Caucasoids, Mongoloids, or Negroids do the Chinese belong? And the Iranians?

(Answers on page 384)

▼ **A woman feeds a yak on the mountain slopes of Nepal. The people of Central Asia often use yaks to carry heavy loads.**

ASIAN NATIONS

	Area in sq. mi	Area in sq. km	Capital	Population
Afghanistan	250,000	647,497	Kabul	18,136,000
Armenia	11,306	29,280	Yerevan	3,300,000
Azerbaijan	33,591	87,000	Baku	7,030,000
Bangladesh	55,598	143,998	Dhaka	113,005,000
Bhutan	18,147	47,000	Thimphu (Thimbu)	1,442,000
Brunei	2,226	5,765	Bandar Seri Begawan	258,000
Cambodia	69,898	181,035	Phnom Penh	8,246,000
China	3,705,408	9,596,961	Beijing	1,121,544,000
Georgia	26,900	69,700	Tbilisi	5,460,000
Hong Kong	403	1,045	Victoria	5,841,000
India	1,269,346	3,287,590	New Delhi	853,373,000
Indonesia	735,139	1,904,000	Jakarta	18,763,000
Japan	145,834	377,708	Tokyo	123,700,000
Kazakhstan	1,049,040	2,717,000	Alma-Ata	16,538,000
Kyrgyzstan	76,838	199,000	Bishkek (Frunze)	4,291,000
Laos	91,429	236,800	Vientiane	4,024,000
Macao	6	16	Macao	514,000
Malaysia	127,317	329,749	Kuala Lumpur	17,886,000
Maldive Islands	115	298	Male	216,000
Mongolia	604,250	1,565,000	Ulan Bator	2,229,000
Myanmar (Burma)	261,218	676,552	Yangon (Rangoon)	41,675,000
Nepal	54,362	140,797	Kathmandu	18,919,000
North Korea	46,540	120,538	Pyongyang	22,937,000
Pakistan	307,374	796,095	Islamabad	122,666,000
Philippines	115,831	300,000	Manila	61,483,000
Singapore	224	581	Singapore City	2,702,000
South Korea	30,025	98,484	Seoul	42,791,000
Sri Lanka	25,332	65,610	Colombo	17,108,000
Taiwan (Formosa)	13,900	36,000	Taipei	20,262,000
Tajikistan	55,213	143,000	Dushanbe	5,112,000
Thailand	198,457	514,000	Bangkok	56,147,000
Turkmenistan	172,974	448,000	Ashkhabad	3,534,000
Uzbekistan	172,588	447,000	Tashkent	19,906,000
Vietnam	127,242	329,556	Hanoi	66,111,000

(Note—for information on southwestern Asian nations see the tables with the articles on ARABIA and MIDDLE EAST. For information on Russia see the table with the article on EUROPE.)

The wet, tropical regions of Asia have many kinds of insects, some of which carry serious diseases. Mosquitoes, which spread malaria, thrive in southern Asia.

People

The peoples of Asia are often separated from each other by scorching deserts, dense jungles, and rugged mountain ranges. Transportation over land is difficult in some places, even today. It is not surprising that thousands of years ago many groups of people never knew they had neighbors. Separated from each other, the Asian peoples developed different religions, languages, styles of art, forms of goverrmnent, and cultures.

Many Asians are farmers who live in small villages located in river valleys throughout many areas of the continent. These farm families often follow the customs and habits of their ancestors, although new farming methods are changing their lives.

Millions of Asians live in cities built along rivers and around harbors. Waterfronts, marketplaces, and streets are jammed with people, animals, wagons, bicycles, cars, buses, and trucks. In Japan, men called "pushers" pack persons into overcrowded trains and buses. Tokyo, Japan, is the most populous Asian city with more than 11 million people. Other Asian cities with many millions include Shanghai, Beijing, and Hong Kong in China; Calcutta and Bombay in India; and Seoul in South Korea. One Asian out of three lives in a city.

Asia has many types of people, belonging to three main groups, each of which is concentrated in its own section of the continent. *Caucasoids* include the Iranians, Indians, Afghans, Pakistanis, and Arabs. These peoples live in western Asia and the Indian subcontinent. *Mongoloids*, including the Chinese, Koreans, and Japanese, live in the Far East. Finally, small groups of *Negroids* live in the Philippines and the Malay Peninsula.

LANGUAGES. Languages vary so much in Asia, that in some places, the people in one village speak differently from people in a neighboring village only a few miles away. Hindi is the official language of India but less than one-third of people can speak it. Fourteen major languages and hundreds of dialects are spoken in India. The Chinese, Tibetan, Burmese, and Thai languages are related to each other, but a speaker of one of these languages will not always understand the others. Nearly four times as many people speak these languages as live in the U.S. The *Altaic* language family includes Turkish, Mongol, and Manchu. Japanese and Korean may be eastern extensions of the Altaic family. People of Southeast Asia also use many different tongues of the Malayo-Polynesian language family. These include Malay, Javanese, Tagalog, and Balinese.

RELIGION. In this vast continent, with so many peoples and ways of living, there are several religions.

All of the world's major religions began in Asia. Hinduism and Buddhism started in India, Judaism and Christianity in the Middle East, Islam in Arabia, Confucianism and Taoism in China, and Shintoism in Japan. These religions have hundreds of millions of followers, and all of them have helped shape the history of the world.

▲ A colorful floating market in Bangkok, the capital of Thailand. Fruit and vegetables are paddled in from the countryside to be sold at the market.

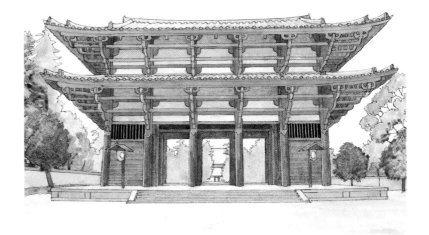

Natural Resources
Asia has both rich and poor soil. Its total farm production is the world's highest, but millions of Asians sometimes go hungry. Millions of tons of rice—the most important Asian crop—are grown each year. Rice plants are usually set into flooded

▲ Buddhism originated in India but spread all over Asia. This Buddhist temple building in Japan was built in the Chinese style.

▲ Young shoots of rice are grown in flooded fields called *paddies*. Every inch of farmland is put to use by cutting out terraces from hillsides.

fields, called *paddies*. Wheat is grown instead of rice in parts of China, Siberia, and in the Indian subcontinent where less rain falls. Huge plantations in Southeast Asia grow enormous crops of rubber, tea, coffee, sugar, and spices. Most of these crops are exported to other continents.

Huge timber forests cover part of Siberia. Exotic woods, such as teak and sandalwood, are shipped all over the world from the tropical forests of Southeast Asia. In some areas, cutting down the forests has caused problems of land erosion.

Fish is a major food of many Asians. Commerical fishing is very important and highly developed in some Asian countries. The annual fish catch of Japan is the greatest in the world. Asia is rich in many mineral resources. One-half of all the known oil reserves in the world are in Southwest Asia, mostly in the countries around the Persian Gulf. Borneo and Indonesia in Southeast Asia also have valuable oil fields. Many other minerals, such as bauxite, chromium, coal, copper, iron, manganese, and tin, are found in large quantities in parts of Asia.

Asia had no important industry until the 1900s. But now Japan is one of the leading industrial powers in the world. India and China are also building many new factories that produce steel, farm equipment, and fertilizer. Other countries, such as the Republic of Korea, are producing many goods, including cars, textiles, and electronic parts. Because workers' wages are low, Asian-made goods are often less expensive than those made elsewhere in the world.

Ancient and Modern

Asia has probably been home to humans for at least 500,000 years. Scientists have found traces of early people in Asia. A skull, called *Peking Man,* is one of the oldest fossils found in human history. The skull was found near Beijing (Peking), China, in 1929. The oldest cities in the world were built in Asia more than 4,000 years ago. One such ancient civilization was in the Indus River Valley of present-day Pakistan.

▶ This is how the ancient city of Mohenjo-Daro in the Indus Valley probably looked at the height of its prosperity. It was built of red bricks and stood on a grid pattern like modern U.S. cities.

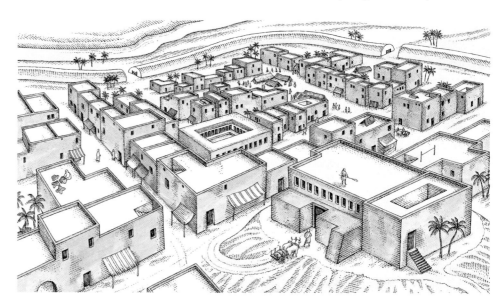

Other ancient civilizations appeared about the same time in other parts of the continent. China had perhaps the greatest ancient civilization of all.

Many of these great civilizations were ravaged in the 13th century by hordes of Mongols, tribes who came from central Asia. The Mongol Empire once extended all the way from China to the Black Sea. Turkish armies took over some areas after the Mongols left.

The riches of Asia—silks, spices, and jewels—attracted traders and explorers from Europe. Starting in the 1500s, many European countries claimed parts of Asia as colonies. China and Japan feared Europe and closed their ports to most foreigners. In the 19th century, Western nations negotiated treaties that opened Asian ports to foreign trade. India came under the control of the British government in 1858, and other Western nations colonized other parts of Asia. France, for example, colonized East Indochina, now Vietnam.

Hundreds of millions of Asians gained freedom from Western colonial rule after World War II. They include Indians, Pakistanis, Burmese, Filipinos, Indonesians, Malaysians, and Indochinese. Hong Kong is a British colony until it is returned to China in 1997; Macao, a Portugese overseas province, will be returned to China in 1999.

The People's Republic of China has a Communist government. In recent years contacts with the West have increased but pro-democracy demonstrations have been put down. The most economically advanced country in Asia, Japan, is a constitutional monarchy. India is the world's most populous nation with a democratic form of government. Like almost everything else, political forms are varied in this largest and most populous continent.

▶▶▶▶ FIND OUT MORE ◀◀◀◀

Arts see Art History; Folk Art; Musical Instruments; Oriental Art; Pagoda; Taj Mahal
History see Ancient Civilizations; Chiang Kai-Shek; Chou En-Lai; Gandhi, Indira; Gandhi, Mahatma; Genghis Khan; Mao Zedong; Nehru, Jawaharlal; Polo, Marco; Sun Yat-Sen
Language see Arabic; Chinese; Languages; Russian
Human Life see Civilization; Human Being
Physical Features see Aral Sea; Arctic; Beijing; Black Sea; Caucasus Mountains; Desert; Ganges River; Gobi Desert; Himalaya Mountains; Middle East; Shanghai; Southeast Asia
Also read the article on each country shown in the table.

◀ **A Japanese "bullet train" speeds through the mountainous countryside. These modern electric trains are among the most technologically advanced in the world.**

▼ **Asia's most powerful industrial nation is Japan. No other country makes as many ships, televisions, CD players, videos, cassette recorders, and cameras. Tokyo, Japan's capital, is a busy and crowded city.**

When John F. Kennedy was assassinated in 1963, a strange tradition continued. Every American President since William H. Harrison who was elected in a year ending in "0" has died while still in office. Harrison was elected in 1840, Abraham Lincoln in 1860, James A. Garfield in 1880, William McKinley in 1900, Warren G. Harding in 1920, Franklin D. Roosevelt in 1940, and John F. Kennedy in 1960. Ronald Reagan, elected in 1980, broke this tradition.

Assyrian kings collected large libraries of clay tablets with cuneiform writing. King Ashurbanipal's large library, discovered in the 1800s, had tablets on medicine, history, religion, literature, and many other subjects.

ASSASSINATION

When a person murders a president, a king, or some other important person, the crime is often called an *assassination*. The murderer is called an *assassin*.

These words came from a group of Muslims who lived more than 900 years ago in Syria and Persia. Before being sent to kill an enemy, a man was always given the drug *hashish* to make him crazy and reckless. From the Arabic name for these men, *hashshashin*, comes the English word "assassin."

An assassin may give different reasons for his crime. He or she may kill for revenge—to punish the victim for some harm (real or imagined) done to the assassin. An assassin may kill a government leader, either because he thinks the leader is evil, or because he wishes to take over control of the government himself. An assassin may even be paid to kill someone. Whatever the reason, most assassins are *fanatics* who believe that whatever they do must be right.

Assassins have killed four United States Presidents—

Abraham Lincoln, James Garfield, William McKinley, and John F. Kennedy. Others tried but failed to assassinate Presidents Andrew Jackson, Theodore Roosevelt, Franklin D. Roosevelt, Harry Truman, Gerald R. Ford, and Ronald Reagan.

▶▶▶▶ **FIND OUT MORE** ◀◀◀◀
Caesar, Julius; Gandhi, Indira; Gandhi, Mahatma; Garfield, James A.; Kennedy, John F.; King, Martin Luther Jr.; Lincoln, Abraham; Malcolm X; McKinley, William; Terrorism

ASSYRIA

Assyria was an ancient kingdom on the upper Tigris River in the country now known as Iraq. Assyrians were great warriors. They invented iron weapons and, by expert strategy, conquered Babylonia to the south, Syria and Israel to the west, and northern Egypt in the 800s and 700s B.C. (See the map with the article on ANCIENT CIVILIZATIONS.) The

▶ The Assyrians were experts at siege warfare. They had battering rams that could knock holes in walls and scaling ladders and towers that helped the warriors climb over the walls.

Assyrian Empire lasted only until 612 B.C., when Babylonia and Media conquered it.

Assyria's main god was Assur, the god of war. Assyria's religion, arts, and customs were mostly borrowed from the Babylonians. Military power was very important to the Assyrians. Merchants' caravans that crossed the Tigris River were charged tolls to pay for the Assyrian armies. King Sennacherib built the Assyrian capital Nineveh about 700 B.C. He made it a magnificent armed camp. The laws of Assyria were harsh. Sometimes as punishment, entire tribes were forced to move to another part of the empire.

Many pieces of Assyrian art from the empire period have been found. Most of their sculpture was done in *relief*, which is shallow carving on stone. Figures of kings and gods were carved on the walls of buildings. Whole walls were used to show scenes of the Assyrian conquest. Some scenes were cruel. Among the most famous sculptures are the large Winged Bulls, which stood before the king's palace to impress visitors.

▶▶▶▶ **FIND OUT MORE** ◀◀◀◀
Ancient Civilizations; Babylonia; Iraq; Mesopotamia; Syria; Tigris and Euphrates rivers

Asteroids were discovered almost by accident. Eighteenth-century astronomers believed there was a planet in an *orbit*, or path, between Mars and Jupiter. By 1800, a great search was underway to locate the new planet. On January 1, 1801, an Italian astronomer, Giuseppe Piazzi, spotted a small dot of light that he had never seen before. He named it Ceres. It was too small to be the missing planet, but astronomers soon decided that Ceres was in orbit where the planet should be.

The mystery was solved when astronomers discovered more asteroids orbiting near Ceres. Instead of one large planet, over 3,000 tiny ones have been found. Many are only one or two miles (2–3 km) across. A few asteroids pass closer to the sun than the inner planet Mercury, while another, Chiron, is farther away than Saturn.

Some of the asteroids may be fragments of two or more small planets that collided and broke up. Others may be tiny embryonic planets that never grew larger. But even if all the asteroids were collected together, they would make a body much smaller than the moon.

▲ The orbit of this asteroid is crossing the Earth's orbit. Asteroids are not round like planets but have a very irregular, bumpy surface.

▼ Most asteroids move around the sun in a wide belt between the orbits of Mars and Jupiter. But some asteroids (shown in the diagram) have erratic orbits that take them beyond the asteroid belt.

ASTEROIDS

The thousands of chunks of metal and rock, which circle the sun between the orbits of the planets Mars and Jupiter, are called *asteroids*, or minor planets.

Only a few of them are large enough to be seen without a powerful telescope. The largest, Ceres, is only 620 miles (998 km) in diameter. Earth's moon has a diameter 3½ times that size.

Planetary Orbits

Orbits of asteroids outside belt

Hidalgo

Eros

Icarus

Asteroid belt

Sun

Earth

Ceres

Mercury

Venus

Mars

Adonis

Jupiter

▶▶▶▶ **FIND OUT MORE** ◀◀◀◀
Solar System

⛩ ASTROLOGY

Astrology is the belief that the movements of the planets, stars, moon, and sun affect people's lives. Astrologers were among the first people to measure the movements of the heavenly bodies. They helped start the science of astronomy.

▼ **This old engraving shows all the star signs of the zodiac, plus other constellations such as Andromeda. Can you find your birth sign?**

Ancient people often used astrology in their religion. Chaldeans and Babylonians believed that the stars caused events and actions to happen here on Earth. The priests said that each person's life depended on the positions of the planets when the person was born. A person's future was decided at the moment of his or her birth. The priests claimed they could tell their king's future. If the planets were in "bad" positions, the country would have trouble. Plans were made for weddings and wars only after checking first with astrologers.

Astrology is based on the *zodiac*, the imaginary circle in the sky in which the sun, moon, and planets move. Also in this circle are 12 constellations, or groups of stars that look like different shapes. Each shape is a *sign* of the zodiac, or a month in the astrologer's calendar.

After learning a person's birth date, an astrologer makes a *horoscope*. This is a map of where the sun and planets within the constellations were on the birth date. From a horoscope, an astrologer tries to tell what will happen to a person in the near future. Astrologers believe that people born under each sign of the zodiac have special character traits.

Astrology is still practiced today. Some people will not make a major decision without a prediction from an astrologer. Many others think astrology is just fun or a lot of nonsense.

▶▶▶▶ **FIND OUT MORE** ◀◀◀◀
Astronomy; Constellation; Mythology

YOUR BIRTHDAY	YOUR SIGN OF THE ZODIAC	
January 21–February 19	Aquarius, the Water Bearer	
February 20–March 20	Pisces, the Fish	
March 21–April 20	Aries, the Ram	
April 21–May 22	Taurus, the Bull	
May 23–June 21	Gemini, the Twins	
June 22–July 22	Cancer, the Crab	
July 23–August 22	Leo, the Lion	
August 23–September 22	Virgo, the Virgin	
September 23–October 22	Libra, the Scales	
October 23–November 21	Scorpio, the Scorpion	
November 22–December 22	Sagittarius, the Archer	
December 23–January 20	Capricorn, the Sea Goat	

🚀 ASTRONAUT

Alan B. Shepard Jr., in his *Freedom 7* spacecraft, was launched into space from Cape Canaveral, Florida, by a Redstone rocket on May 5, 1961. Shepard was the first American in space. He was also one of America's first seven astronauts. The others were Virgil I. Grissom, Donald K. Slayton, John H. Glenn Jr., Malcolm S. Carpenter, Walter M. Schirra, and Leroy G. Cooper Jr.

Astronaut comes from the Greek

words *astron,* "star" and *nautes,* "sailor." In the former Soviet Union, astronauts are called *cosmonauts.* A Soviet cosmonaut, Yuri Gagarin, was the first person to travel in space on April 12, 1961. Since then people from many countries, including England, Canada, France, India, Syria, and Vietnam have flown in space. The first woman in space was Valentina Tereshkova in 1963. Neil Armstrong and Edwin Aldrin Jr. made the first landing on the moon in July 1969. In June 1971, cosmonauts launched the first manned space station. During a 24-day mission, three cosmonauts lived in space and performed scientific studies. The first scientist astronaut was geologist Harrison Schmitt, who went to the moon in 1972.

The U.S. also launched a manned space station, *Skylab,* in 1973. It was used in turn by three crews sent up in Apollo spacecraft. They used cameras and a space telescope to study the Earth and the sun. One crew stayed for 84 days, breaking a record.

Extra vehicular activity (EVA) suit

Hand controls

Manned maneuvering unit (MMU)

Astronauts are trained by the National Aeronautics and Space Administration (NASA), in Houston, Texas. Those who cannot fly spend a year learning to fly jets. Astronauts begin general training when they can fly, then learn about mechanics, guidance and control, communication, navigation, astronomy, and geology.

Each astronaut is assigned to a crew and trains for one special job to be done during a space flight. These astronauts fly jet trainers in practice sessions at least three times a week and spend thousands of hours "flying" in *simulators.* Simulators are special training machines and equipment that look and operate like real spacecraft equipment. In the simula-

tors, astronauts learn to pilot the spacecraft. They learn how every piece of equipment works; how to *navigate,* or control the course of the spacecraft; how to handle emergencies; and how it feels to be weightless. They also learn to perform experiments, take photographs, and walk in space.

After Skylab, the U.S. space program concentrated on building a returnable spacecraft. They built the space shuttle, which can carry up to five passengers and two crew members. It has taken non-astronaut civilians into orbit around Earth. Each flight has performed scientific experiments and new technological feats. In 1986, the space shuttle *Challenger* exploded shortly after takeoff. One of the passengers was teacher Sharon Christa McAuliffe.

In 1990, the former Soviet Union began taking paying passengers aboard its space station, *Mir,* meaning "peace." One of the passengers was biologist Helen Sharman, who became the first Briton in space in May 1991.

▶ ▶ ▶ ▶ **FIND OUT MORE** ◀ ◀ ◀ ◀
Armstrong, Neil; Gagarin, Yuri; Glenn, John; Shepard, Alan B.; Space Travel

▲ **There is no gravity in space, so astronauts experience weightlessness. These astronaut candidates are learning how it feels to be weightless by using a special training machine.**

◀ **A jet-powered backpack, called a manned maneuvering unit, allows an astronaut to move in space without a safety line. For work outside the spacecraft an astronaut wears an extra vehicular activity suit.**

▼ **A doctor takes a sample of blood from an astronaut on board the space shuttle. He will use the blood to investigate the effects of weightlessness on astronauts.**

▲ A Mesopotamian "star map." Three thousand years old, this stone tablet shows the constellation Scorpio as well as the moon and the planet Venus.

▶ Medieval astronomers sought ways of measuring time using heavenly bodies. Here they are comparing the lunar (moon) year with the solar (sun) year.

▼ During the early Middle Ages, Arab astronomers drew the constellations as human figures (as the Greeks before them had done). This one is called Cepheus.

ASTRONOMY

People have always looked up at the sky and asked questions about what they saw. What makes the sun shine? What makes it warm? What are the stars, the moon, the planets? Astronomers are the people who try to answer these questions. Astronomy is the study of the *heavenly bodies,* all the objects in the sky and of the universe as a whole. It is the oldest science.

One task of astronomy is to keep track of all the heavenly bodies. What time will the sun rise? What time will it set? When will winter begin? When will it be warm enough to plant crops? These questions were very important to the first astronomers. They are still important to farmers, sailors, pilots, astronauts, and many other people.

Ancient astronomers studied the objects in the sky for a very long time. They finally began to notice *patterns*—events that happened again and again. One important pattern they saw was the *phases of the moon.* If you look at the moon every night for a month, you will see the changes, or phases, it goes through. At the beginning of the pattern, the moon does not shine. The next night, it looks like a very thin piece of a circle. We call both of these shapes the *new moon.* Each night for a week, the curved, shiny piece grows bigger. At the end of the week, a half circle glows in the sky. Two weeks after the new moon, we see the *full moon,* a bright, shiny circle. Then, every night for two weeks, less and less of the circle shows. Finally, the moon disappears again. We are back to the start of the pattern, the new moon.

Astronomers invented the first calendar using this pattern. Early calendars were not as accurate as the calendars of today. But they helped farmers and sailors, just as today's calendars help people.

Astronomers in the ancient world could measure many things that happened in the sky, but they could not explain why these things happened. The second main task of astronomy is to explain the reasons for events in the sky. The ancient Chinese built a big observatory some 4,600 years ago. They could predict when eclipses would occur, but they did not know how to explain what happened. The darkness scared them. People believed an eclipse happened because a dragon tried to swallow the sun. People in many different countries made up *myths,* or imaginary stories, to explain events in the sky they could not understand. Ancient Greek astronomers made the most progress in explaining how some things happen in the sky.

Greek Astronomy

The most difficult problem was to explain how and why the heavenly bodies seemed to circle the Earth. Pythagoras, in the 500s B.C., and then Aristarchus, three centuries later, taught that the planets revolved around the sun. But not many people believed them. Plato and Aristotle, two important philosophers and astronomers, taught that the Earth is the center of the universe. They thought the sun, moon, stars, and planets were attached to giant *spheres,* or transparent shells, which rotated around the Earth. This seemed easier to believe. Claudius Ptolemy, a Greek who lived in Egypt around A.D. 100–170, believed what Aristotle and Plato taught. He wrote 13 books that he believed proved the Earth is the center of the universe. For centuries many other people thought he was right.

Nicolaus Copernicus, a Polish astronomer who lived in the 1500s, claimed that all the planets revolved around the sun. Again, people said he was wrong. But a few astronomers listened to him and made great discoveries. In the late 1500s, a Danish astronomer, Tycho Brahe, measured the movements of all the heavenly bodies he could see. Brahe made careful records. Johannes Kepler, a German scientist, used Brahe's measurements to show that the Earth and all other planets *orbit* the sun. Galileo, an Italian, verified this fact after he started using a telescope.

Modern Astronomy

The telescope was the tool that finally helped astronomers understand the movements of the heavenly bodies. Even a small telescope made a great difference. Galileo was the first astronomer to use one. It was not very powerful when compared to today's telescopes, but by using this tool, he was able to see things that no one had ever seen before.

In 1610, Galileo discovered four moons belonging to Jupiter (Jupiter really has at least 17 moons, but the others are so small Galileo could not see them with his weak telescope). When he saw these four moons orbiting around Jupiter, Galileo knew that Aristotle was wrong to say that everything in the universe revolves around the Earth. He also discovered that the planet Venus must revolve around the sun, as the moon revolves around us, because we can see the different phases of Venus in the same way we see different phases of the moon.

More than 375 years have passed since Galileo's discovery. Scientists have been making bigger and better telescopes since Galileo first used one. Astronomers now have other important tools, too. A camera is as important as a telescope to today's

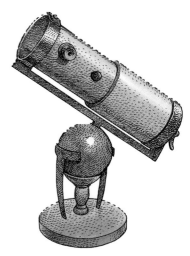

◄ A diagram showing the Greek astronomer Ptolemy's theory of the solar system. He described the Earth at the center surrounded by water, air, and fire.

▲ Issac Newton built the first reflector telescope in 1668. Stars seen through early telescopes had fuzzy edges, but Newton's telescope corrected this.

LEARN BY DOING

You can "discover" the moon just as ancient astronomers did. Begin with a full moon. Note what time it rises by keeping a daily time chart by your clock. Does your time agree with the time shown in the newspaper? Study the moon's details with a telescope or binoculars (remember ancient astronomers did not have these tools). Keep a daily record from one full moon to the next.

If clouds hide the moon, guess how it would look. Record that you did not see the moon and check your guess by watching the next cycle. You may have to make several observations to see all the moon's phases.

As the moon circles the Earth, it hides several stars—Aldebaran, Regulus, Spica, Antares, and the Pleiades. Try to watch an *occultation* (hiding), noting down how long it lasts.

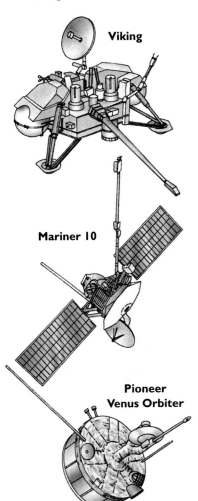

▲ Optical telescopes can be very large, but interference from the Earth's atmosphere limits how much astronomers can see through them.

Viking

Mariner 10

Pioneer Venus Orbiter

◀ Astronomers use space probes to reveal more about our solar system. By using probes they can get a closer look at the planets. The three shown here have, among them, visited the planets Mars, Venus, and Mercury.

astronomer. Astronomers often use them together. They take special photographs called *time exposures*. To make these photographs, the light of stars is allowed to shine on the film for hours instead of just part of a second. These photographs reveal stars whose light is too faint to see, even with a telescope. Astronomers often discover comets and asteroids by accident on time exposures. A comet or asteroid shows up on film as a line of light. Stars look like dots.

Another important tool is the *spectrograph*. It examines and separates a ray of light into the different colors in it. When light from a star shines through a spectrograph, an expert looks to see how much of each color is in the light. He can tell what a star is made of by looking at the different colors in the spectrum.

Many objects in the universe send out radio waves. These were first detected, accidentally, in 1932, and since that time radio astronomers have made many important discoveries. For example, the space between stars in the galaxy contains very fine,

scattered dust, which blocks out light from other objects beyond. But radio waves sent out by these objects can pass through the dust and be received by radio telescopes. Some of the most distant galaxies in the universe send out radio waves very strongly. Radio telescopes usually have a big curved metal dish to focus the radio waves they receive.

Today's astronomers use the tools of radio astronomy, X-ray astronomy, and space travel. Manmade orbiting satellites and rockets fly above the Earth's atmosphere. Here they can take clearer photographs of the sun and planets than can be taken from ground level, through the Earth's atmosphere. Astronauts have walked on the moon; space probes have flown past other planets. Probes have landed on Mercury, Venus, and Mars and have flown by the outer planets, such as Jupiter and Uranus.

The Universe

No one knew the size of the universe in ancient times. Ptolemy knew that stars are farther away from Earth than the planets are. But if you could talk to Ptolemy and tell him how far away the stars really are, or how far even the planets are, he would probably not believe you. They are so distant that astronomers have had to invent new units of measurement.

If you said that New York and San Francisco are about 190,080,000 inches (482,803,200 cm) apart, you would be right. But this would confuse most people, because the number is too large to understand easily. This is one reason people use *miles* or *kilometers* as a unit of measure. People usually say the two cities are about 3,000 miles (4,830 km) apart. Astronomers have the same problem except more so. Distances in space are so great that even miles or kilometers do not tell how far away the objects are. So astronomers use other measuring units. To measure distances inside the *solar system* (the sun and its nine planets), astronomers use the *astronomical unit* (a.u.). One a.u. is the mean distance from Earth to the sun, about 93 million miles (150 million km). Astronomers say Pluto is about 39 a.u. from the sun. This is easier than saying 3,670,000,000 miles.

The first accurate measurement of the distance to the stars was made in 1838. It was discovered that even the nearest star is a quarter of a million times as far away as the sun. This means that if an orange in New York represents the sun in size, then another orange representing its neighbor would have to be placed in Las Vegas, Nevada. Astronomical units are much too small for these huge spaces, so astronomers measure the distances between the stars in *light-years* (the distance that light travels in a year). Light travels about 186,000 miles (300,000 km) a second, or 5,870,000,000,000 miles (9,461,000,000,000 km) a year. Light from the stars travels a long time to reach the Earth. The nearest star to Earth is Alpha Centauri. Its light takes about four years and four months to travel the distance to Earth. Even light from the sun takes about eight minutes to journey to Earth.

The sun is an average kind of star. It belongs, with about 100 billion other stars, to the Milky Way *galaxy*. A galaxy is a huge group of stars, which may be much hotter or cooler than the sun, and much larger or smaller. All the stars seen in the night sky belong to our galaxy. Looking out into space, millions of other galaxies come into view as faint smudges of light. Some of these contain ten times as many stars as our own, but others may have only a hundredth as many.

Astronomers can now see at least

10 billion light-years away from Earth. At this huge distance, only the very powerful galaxies known as *quasars* are bright enough to be seen. All distant galaxies are being carried away from our own galaxy at thousands of miles a second, because the universe is expanding. If their speeds and distances are calculated backward, it looks as if all the galaxies in the universe were close together between approximately 15 and 20 billion years ago. Most astronomers believe that this is when the *Big Bang* occurred, and that the atomic particles that form everything, from microbes to galaxies, came into existence in one amazing explosion. As astronomers develop bigger and better telescopes, they see farther and farther out into space and learn more and more about our amazing universe.

▲ **IRAS (Infra-Red Astronomy Satellite) was launched in 1983 to collect information on infrared radiation given off by distant stars and galaxies.**

▶▶▶▶ **FIND OUT MORE** ◀◀◀◀

Astronomers see Brahe, Tycho; Copernicus, Nicolaus; Einstein, Albert; Galileo; Herschel Family; Kepler, Johannes; Newton, Issac

Astronomers at Work see Light; Observatory; Planetarium; Radio Astronomy; Space Research; Spectrum; Statistics; Telescope

Beyond the Solar System see Constellation; Milky Way; North Star; Star; Universe

History see Astrology; Calendar; Earth History

Solar System see Asteroid; Comets; Eclipse; Gravity and Gravitation; Meteor; Moon; Radiation Belt; Solar System; Sun

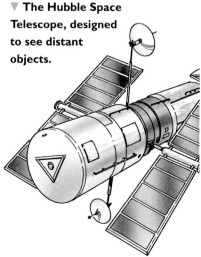

▼ **The Hubble Space Telescope, designed to see distant objects.**

▲ Originally a fort, the Acropolis at Athens was completely transformed in the 5th century B.C. into a complex of spectacular shrines and temples.

▲ Athens was famous for its painted pottery.

ATHENS

Greece's largest city, cultural center, and capital is Athens. It stands on the plain of Attica, between the mountains and the Aegean Sea. Piraeus, its port, is but a few miles away. Athens is one of the world's great historic cities. The art, literature, philosophy, and law of ancient Athens form much of the basis of Western culture and civilization. Today, scholars and tourists come to view remains of the city's ancient history.

Athens was built around a flat-topped hill called the *Acropolis*. This hill was first a fortress to which Athenians fled in case of attack by enemies. Later, beautiful temples were built on the Acropolis in honor of

Greek gods and goddesses. The *Parthenon*, one of these temples, is regarded as one of the finest examples of architecture ever built. The public square and marketplace, called the *Agora*, lay to the northwest of the Acropolis. In the fifth century B.C., Athens reached the peak of its cultural achievement.

Writers of long ago described the Athenians as people who loved the art of living more than they loved wealth and power. The modern city is much larger than the Athens of old. Its fine public buildings and museums show visitors that Athenians still take pride in their glorious past.

▶▶▶▶ **FIND OUT MORE** ◀◀◀◀
Acropolis; City; Greece; Greece, Ancient

ATHLETICS

SEE OLYMPIC GAMES; SPORTS; TRACK AND FIELD

ATLANTIC OCEAN

The Atlantic Ocean stretches from the Arctic Circle to Antarctica. It washes the shores of five continents and is the second largest body of water in the world. North America, South America, Europe, Africa, and Antarctica all border on the Atlantic. Many large gulfs and seas are "arms" of the Atlantic. These arms on the west coast of the Atlantic are Baffin Bay, Hudson Bay, the Gulf of Mexico, and the Caribbean Sea. On the east, the arms of the Atlantic include the Baltic Sea, North Sea, Bay of Biscay, Mediterranean Sea, and the Gulf of Guinea.

◀ Leif Eriksson, a Viking from Iceland, is thought to be the first European to have crossed the Atlantic Ocean. He sailed from Greenland to North America about A.D. 1000.

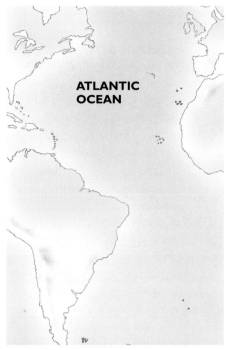

ATLANTIC
OCEAN

The largest islands found in the Atlantic area are in the North Atlantic, the part north of the equator. These include Newfoundland, Greenland, Iceland, the British Isles, Cuba in the Caribbean, and the Azores, west of Portugal. The South Atlantic has fewer islands. The largest southern islands are the Falklands, east of South America's southern tip.

Several *currents* move through the Atlantic. The *Gulf Stream* is the best known current. It carries warm water north along the east coast of North America and then east to Europe. The *Labrador Current* brings cold water from the Arctic to the shores of eastern North America. The *Brazil Current* flows south along the east coast of South America before turning east.

Tall underwater mountains rise from the bottom of the Atlantic. Deep trenches or valleys lie in between the mountains. Open plains form islands that sometimes rise above the ocean surface. The *Mid-Atlantic Ridge* is a chain of mountains running from Iceland southward almost to the tip of South America. This ridge is expanding, or spreading out sideways, very slowly. Thus, North and South America are slowly being pushed farther from Europe and Africa.

Deep valleys lie on the ocean floor. The *Puerto Rico Trench* is on the western edge of the Atlantic Ocean. It is 27,510 feet (8,385 m) deep. Other shallow valleys that look like riverbeds crisscross the wide, flat plains that extend on both sides of the undersea mountains.

The ancient Egyptians were probably the first explorers of the Atlantic. They sailed the Mediterranean and South Atlantic. Later the Phoenicians sailed the Mediterranean past Gibraltar up the North Atlantic to England and Scandinavia. The Vikings were perhaps the first to cross the Atlantic to the New World, about a thousand years ago. The people who led the way to permanent European settlements along the western Atlantic shore, however, were Christopher Columbus and the explorers who followed him. John W. Alcock and Arthur W. Brown were the first to fly nonstop across the Atlantic, in 1919. In 1927, Charles Lindbergh was the first to *solo*, or fly alone, across the Atlantic. Some of today's jet airplanes, such as the Concorde, can fly across the Atlantic in less than three hours.

▶▶▶▶ **FIND OUT MORE** ◀◀◀◀
Exploration; Gulf Stream; Lindbergh, Charles; Maury, Matthew; Ocean; Seacoast; Tide

▼ The granite cliffs of Land's End, the most westerly point in Britain, are typical of the rugged beauty of North Atlantic coastlines.

▲ This picture of a volcano exploding shows the immense natural power that may have been responsible for destroying the lost kingdom of Atlantis.

▼ A section from the Catalan Atlas of 1375, showing the detailed mapping techniques of the time.

ATLANTIS

The story of Atlantis comes from the myths of ancient times. Plato, a famous philosopher who lived in ancient Greece, wrote about this powerful kingdom. He said that Atlantis was a large island in the Atlantic Ocean, somewhere west of the Pillars of Hercules (the Rock of Gibraltar). Supposedly Atlantis had great armies that invaded many countries around the Mediterranean Sea about 12,000 years ago. Plato said that the ancient Greeks of Athens defeated the armies of Atlantis. Some time after that, giant storms and earthquakes destroyed the island because, as legends say, the people of Atlantis were evil.

Atlantis may never have existed. Its ruins have never been located. But archeologists think it may have been an ancient Mediterranean civilization, flooded after a terrible volcanic eruption. The Aegean island of Thera (Santorini), which suddenly blew up about 3,500 years ago, led to such a theory. Plato's story could have come from tales that explorers told about real islands they visited in their travels. Perhaps someone will find the remains of glorious Atlantis one day.

▶▶▶▶ **FIND OUT MORE** ◀◀◀◀
Legend; Mythology

ATLAS

A Flemish mapmaker, Gerardus Mercator, was the first to call a book of maps an atlas. In 1585 he named his book of maps after the Greek god, Atlas, because of the old custom of putting a picture of Atlas on the first page of a map book. The Greeks believed that Atlas held the world on his shoulders.

Ancient atlases look strange today. Mapmakers knew little about most of the world's land masses until the 1500s. European mapmakers had to guess at the shape and size of continents other than Europe. They also had very few maps to help them. Maps began to improve as people explored more and more of the world.

Today's atlases contain many maps. A world atlas is usually the biggest type of atlas. World atlases have information about the climate, the natural resources, and the high and low places of each country. The first map in a world atlas generally pictures the whole world. Next come maps of the continents: North America, South America, Africa, Europe, Asia, Australia, and Antarctica. A detailed map of almost every country in the world is included in a world atlas. Each map shows the cities, lakes, rivers, deserts, and mountains of the country. An atlas of the United States shows maps of every state in detail. Special atlases may tell about the history of various countries, the products they grow and manufacture, their plant life, or how their boundaries have changed through history. Atlases may have *gazetteers*, which is a section with lists of names of cities, rivers, mountains, lakes, and deserts, and directions for finding them on the maps.

Countries and cities grow larger or smaller and sometimes change their names. Borders between countries may change through agreement or wars. People who make atlases must

constantly bring them up to date. A modern aid to accurate mapmaking is photography from the air and from satellites in space. This is one reason why modern atlases are better than old ones. An atlas is included in *Young Students Learning Library*. Use it to read articles about countries.

▶▶▶▶ **FIND OUT MORE** ◀◀◀◀
Exploration; Map

ATMOSPHERE

Air surrounds the ball-shaped Earth like a transparent shell. This wrapping of air is the *atmosphere.* You could not live without it and the oxygen it contains. It keeps out some harmful rays from the sun. It also keeps the Earth's temperature moderate. The moon, which has no air, has temperatures of 250°F (121°C) during the day and −280°F (−173°C) at night!

Although the atmosphere surrounds the Earth, it does not have a definite thickness as the skin of a grapefruit does. It just gets thinner and thinner. It is divided into four layers. The lowest layer, the *troposphere,* holds most of the air people and other living things breathe. It also provides the conditions to make weather. Weather is the result of changing conditions. For example, clouds cover the sky and cause rain or snow. The troposphere is not very thick—about 10 miles (16 km) thick over the equator and about 5 miles (8 km) thick over the North Pole and the South Pole. But the troposphere has more molecules of air than all the other atmospheric layers put together.

Air is a mixture of gases. Over three-fourths of air is nitrogen, and almost all the rest is oxygen, with tiny amounts, or *traces,* of other gases. Dust, salt from oceans, water droplets, pollen from plants, soot from factory chimneys, and ashes

from burnt meteors float in the troposphere in the form of vapor, clouds, ice crystals, and rain or snow.

The *stratosphere* is the second layer of the atmosphere. It begins where the troposphere ends and is about 40 miles (64 km) thick. The air is thin and very cold—about −67°F (−55°C) in the lower stratosphere. It is also calm. Jet planes often fly in the lower stratosphere, above wind and rain. In the top part of the troposphere, winds can blow up to 300 miles an hour (480 km/hr.). Scientists call these winds *jet streams.*

The third layer of the atmosphere, the *mesosphere,* begins about

▼ The atmosphere is held close to the Earth by gravity. It is divided into various layers according to differences in temperature.

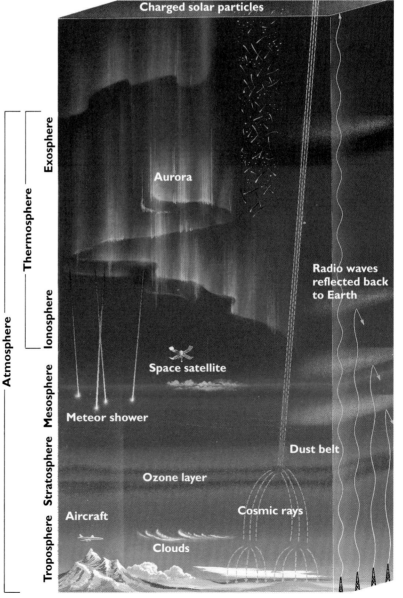

The mixture of gases in the atmosphere has taken more than 4.5 billion years to evolve. About 99 percent of the atmosphere is made up of nitrogen and oxygen. The gases in the remaining 1 percent are argon, carbon dioxide and tiny amounts of hydrogen, ozone, methane, carbon monoxide, helium, neon, krypton and xenon.

50 miles (80 km) above Earth and reaches upward about 350 miles (560 km). It includes a region that scientists call the *ionosphere,* because it contains many electrically charged particles called *ions.* Air molecules are very far apart in this layer, but they do help protect the Earth from meteors and from strong rays of the sun.

Some important things happen in the ionosphere. Flickering lights sometimes shine there. In the Northern Hemisphere, these lights are called the *Aurora Borealis,* or northern lights. The southern lights are called the *Aurora Australis.* Meteors, or falling stars, start to burn up in the ionosphere, about 70 to 80 miles (113 to 129 km) above Earth. The bottom of the ionosphere reflects (bounces) radio signals back to Earth, enabling messages to be sent around the curved surface of the Earth. If this did not happen, all radio waves would shoot off into space.

Above the ionosphere is the *exosphere,* which stretches up hundreds of miles. The higher above Earth you go, the fewer air molecules there are in the same amount of space. In the

exosphere the temperature rises again, until it reaches 1,800°F (1,000°C).

Outer space is dark, yet when we look up we see blue sky. Why? The answer is that the atmosphere contains many tiny particles of matter that scatter the light reaching the Earth from the sun. They scatter more of the blue light in the sun's light rays than other colors. So we see a blue sky—when there are no clouds low down in the atmosphere to spoil the view. Other planets and the stars have atmospheres, too. Scientific studies have found that most of these atmospheres probably contain gases that are different from those in the Earth's atmosphere.

▶▶▶▶ **FIND OUT MORE** ◀◀◀◀
Air; Aurora; Meteor; Radio;
Weather

ATOM

Have you ever wondered what would happen if you could cut something smaller and smaller, millions of times? Suppose you had a piece of pure gold. You cut it in half,

▲ A table of chemical elements, drawn by the British scientist John Dalton around 1803. Elements are "pure" substances—all their atoms are the same. Dalton was the first to give elements letters of the alphabet.

▶ The structure of a *neon* atom (atomic weight 20.2, atomic number 10.) An atom consists of a nucleus, which is made up of protons and neutrons, and electrons that constantly spin around the nucleus.

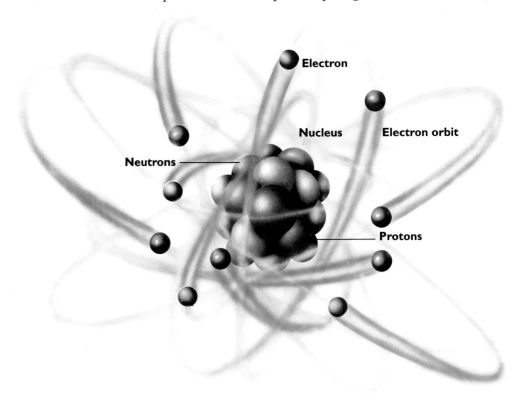

Electron

Nucleus

Electron orbit

Neutrons

Protons

and then cut the half in half. Could you keep on cutting the halves an endless number of times? No. There would come a time when you had a very small piece of gold that could not be cut in half again and still be gold. This very small piece is called an *atom* of gold.

All *matter,* anything that has weight and takes up space, is made up of atoms. The pages of this book and the ink printed on them, a glass and the milk in it, the air you breathe, and all things that can be weighed and measured are made up of various kinds of atoms.

Think of an atom as being round like a ball. If you could put 250 million atoms of average size side by side, they would make up a row one inch (2.5 cm) long. This means that an atom is just one two-hundred-and-fifty-millionth of an inch (11,000 microns) across its widest part, or *diameter.*

There are more than 100 different kinds of atoms. Matter that is made up of only one kind of atom is called an *element.* Atoms of elements combine to make *molecules* of many different kinds of matter. Most elements are found naturally on the Earth, but some have been identified only in laboratories. (See the table of elements in the article on ELEMENT.)

The Idea of Atoms

The idea of atoms is not new. Some 2,400 years ago, scientists in Greece wondered what matter was made of. One named Democritus of Abdera believed that all matter was made up of extremely small, entirely solid particles (very small bits) of different sizes and shapes. These tiny particles could not be split or cut, so Democritus named them *atomos,* which in Greek means "not cuttables." Our word atom came from the Greek word *atomos.*

Over 2,000 years later, in 1808, an English schoolmaster, John Dalton,

put forward an idea like the one of Democritus. Dalton said that matter was made up of tiny, round solid particles called atoms. His ideas of what atoms were and how atoms behaved helped lay the foundation for chemistry.

Inside an Atom

We now know that an atom is not solid but is made up of a number of smaller units known as *subatomic particles.* An atom contains a central part called a *nucleus.* One or more *electrons* revolve around the nucleus. An electron is a particle carrying a negative electric charge. The smallest and lightest atom, the hydrogen atom, has one electron. The largest atoms have more than 100. Electrons revolve around the nucleus in orbits that crisscross in several directions, as shown in the picture. An American

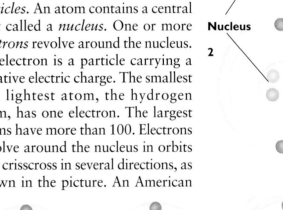

Fluorine atom   Neon atom   Sodium atom

physicist, Robert A. Millikan, was able to weigh electrons. He found that each weighed about one three-quadrillionth of an ounce. (A quadrillion is written as 1,000,000,000,000,000.)

The nucleus of an atom is made up of two kinds of particles: a *proton,* a particle with a positive charge of electricity, and a *neutron* which has no electric charge. (The exception is the smallest and lightest atom, the hydrogen atom. It has no neutrons.)

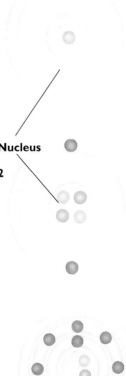

▼ The nucleus of a hydrogen atom (1) has one proton. It has no neutrons. One electron revolves around the nucleus. The nucleus of a helium atom (2) has two protons and two neutrons. Two electrons revolve around the nucleus.

– Stands for an electron
+ Stands for a proton
n Stands for a neutron

1

Nucleus

2

▲ The fluorine atom has two shells. But the second shell has only seven electrons and is therefore not filled. The neon atom also has two shells. But the second shell has eight electrons and is therefore filled. The sodium atom has a third shell, which is only just begun, having one electron.

▼ **Atoms become ions when they gain or lose an electron. The diagram shows how the particles of an ion differ from those of a neutral atom of the same substance.**

Sodium atom   11 Protons
11 Electrons   0 Charge

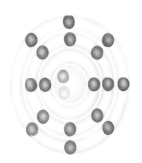

Sodium ion   11 Protons
10 Electrons   +1 Charge

Chlorine atom   17 Protons
17 Electrons   0 Charge

Chlorine ion   17 Protons
18 Electrons   −1 Charge

The weight, or more correctly, the *mass,* of a proton and a neutron are almost equal. The nucleus of a hydrogen atom is more than 1,800 times as heavy as an electron. Although the largest atom has 105 electrons revolving around the nucleus, the combined mass of all these electrons is still a very small part of the total mass of the atom. So the mass of an atom is just about equal to the mass of its nucleus.

The nucleus is very small when compared to the size of an atom. If the diameter of an atom were as long as a football field (100 yards or 91 meters), then the nucleus, on the 50 yard line, would be as big as a pea. So an atom is mostly empty space.

Scientists now know that protons and neutrons themselves are made up of even smaller particles.

Electrons are arranged in orbits in a very definite way. The orbits are called *shells.* The orbit closest to the nucleus can hold only two electrons. This orbit may have only one electron, as it does in a hydrogen atom. But when the orbit has a second electron, as in an atom of helium, the orbit is said to be *filled.* The second orbit from the nucleus can hold 8 electrons; the third, 18; the fourth, 32; and so on.

Ions and Isotopes

Most atoms have an equal number of electrons and protons. This means that they have the same number of positive and negative electric charges. An atom with equal number of positive and negative electric charges acts as if it had no charge at all. It is electrically neutral. But if an atom gains an electron, it will have an extra charge of negative electricity. The atom will be electrically negative. Or, if it loses an electron, it will have more protons than electrons. It will be electrically positive. Atoms that are electrically charged are called *ions.*

When scientists first set about weighing atoms, they decided to say that an oxygen atom is equal to exactly 16 atomic weight units. They then compared the other atoms to oxygen. (Since 1960, carbon, with a weight of 12, has been used as the base instead of oxygen.) The scientists were puzzled by the fact that the weights of the other atoms were not whole numbers. For example, the chlorine atom has a weight of 35.45. Iron weighs 55.85.

When the neutron was discovered, scientists found that not all atoms of the same element have the same number of neutrons. Chlorine atoms, for example, have two different kinds of nuclei. One contains 17 protons and 18 neutrons, and the other has 17 protons and 20 neutrons. The average of large numbers of the two kinds of atoms gives chlorine its atomic weight of 35.45. Atoms of the same element having different numbers of neutrons are called *isotopes.*

▶ ▶ ▶ ▶ **FIND OUT MORE** ◀ ◀ ◀ ◀
Anti-matter; Chemistry; Element; Gas; Liquid; Matter; Nuclear Energy; Quantum; Solid

ATOMIC ENERGY

SEE NUCLEAR ENERGY

ATTILA THE HUN
(about 406–453)

Attila the Hun united the Huns, a tribe of nomadic Asians living in what is now Hungary in eastern Europe. Under his powerful leadership the Huns conquered much of the Roman Empire. Attila was called the "Scourge of God," meaning that he brought punishment.

Attila followed his uncle, Roas, as king of the Huns. Attila first shared the throne with his brother, Bleda, but he later had his brother killed. Attila led his forces from the Danube River to the Mediterranean Sea, killing people and burning villages along the way. Whoever was not killed was forced to serve in Attila's army.

Attila next tried to conquer the Eastern Roman Empire. He could not capture its capital, Constantinople, because of its strong walls. But he forced the city to give him land and pay a large sum of money. Attila invaded Gaul (now France) in A.D. 451 but was stopped by an army of Romans and Visigoths (West Goths) at Chalons, France.

Attila then invaded Italy. He left destruction wherever he went. As Attila neared Rome, Pope Leo I met him and somehow convinced him to turn back. Attila planned to invade Italy again, but he died before he had the opportunity to do so.

▶▶▶▶ **FIND OUT MORE** ◀◀◀◀
Rome, Ancient

AUDUBON, JOHN JAMES (1785–1851)

Birds of all kinds fascinated John James Audubon, and he spent most of his life studying them. Audubon put all the details he observed into beautiful pictures of the birds he studied. His paintings were made into a set of books called *Birds of America.*

Audubon was born in Haiti. His mother, a Haitian, died soon after his birth. His father, a French naval officer, sent him to France to attend school. When he was 18, Audubon went to live on his father's farm near Philadelphia, Pennsylvania. There he spent most of his time drawing birds. Audubon later opened a general store in Kentucky. But he did not do well in business because he spent most of his time drawing.

Audubon tried to sell his paintings of American birds, but no publisher was interested. He went to England in 1826, and at last published his *Birds of America.* He met William McGillivray, a Scottish naturalist,

who edited Audubon's book *Ornithological Biography.* Published in 1938, this book contained observations and paintings of American birds.

Audubon's work made many Americans aware of their native birds. The National Audubon Society is named in his honor. This organization works to protect birds and to teach people nature conservation.

▶▶▶▶ **FIND OUT MORE** ◀◀◀◀
Bird; Conservation

AUGUST

Long ago the month we call August was called *Sextilis*. It was the sixth month in the ancient Roman calendar (the Roman year began in March and only had 10 months). Sextilis was renamed August in 8 B.C. in honor of Augustus Caesar, the first Roman emperor. August is now the eighth month of the year and has 31 days. The poppy and the gladiolus are the flowers of August. August birthstones are the peridot, which is clear green, and the sardonyx, which has brown and white stripes.

Poppy

Sardonyx

▲ **Attila and his Huns terrorized Europe during the A.D. 400s.**

▲ **Audubon's *Blue Jay*; National Gallery of Art, Washington, D.C., gift of Mrs. Walter B. James.**

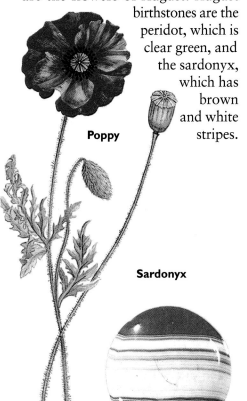

◀ **August's flower is the poppy. People born in August have the sardonyx as their birthstone.**

DATES OF SPECIAL EVENTS IN AUGUST

2	President Warren G. Harding died (1923) and Calvin Coolidge became President.
3	Columbus set sail from Spain on his first voyage to the New World (1492). The *Nautilus* became the first submarine to cross the North Pole underwater (1958).
6	The United States dropped the first atomic bomb on Hiroshima, Japan (1945).
8	The Spanish Armada was defeated by the English Navy (1588). President Richard Nixon resigned on national TV (1974).
9	The United States dropped the second atomic bomb on Nagasaki, Japan (1945).
10	President Herbert Hoover was born (1874).
12	Thomas Edison invented the phonograph (1877).
13	Spanish *conquistadores* (conquerors) captured Mexico City from the Aztecs (1521).
14	World War II ended when Japan surrendered to Allied Forces (1945).
15	The Panama Canal opened to shipping (1914).
17	Davy Crockett, the American frontiersman, was born (1786).
18	Virginia Dare was born—the first child of English parents to be born in America (1587).
20	President Benjamin Harrison was born (1833).
24	The British burned the White House and the Capitol during the War of 1812 (1814).
26	Women were given the right to vote by the passage of the nineteenth amendment to the Constitution (1920).
27	Confucius, the Chinese philosopher, was born (551 B.C.).
28	A great civil rights march on Washington, D.C., led by Reverend Martin Luther King Jr., took place (1963).

August is the peak of summer in the temperate zone of the Northern Hemisphere. The days are apt to be some of the hottest of the year, though the longest days are past. The hot, sultry days of July and August are called "dog days" by many. This is because Sirius, the Dog Star, rises and sets with the sun and shines very clearly and brightly during August.

In far northern Canada and Alaska, chilly nights in August signal the end of summer. In the Southern Hemisphere, warmer winds signal the end of winter in places such as Chile and Argentina.

July and August are popular months for taking summer vacations.

▶▶▶▶ **FIND OUT MORE** ◀◀◀◀
Calendar; Month; Season; Summer

AURORA

The night sky in the far north is often bright with dancing lights of many colors. Rays of light shoot across the sky and then fade. Curtains of light flicker. This beautiful sight is called the *Aurora Borealis*, the northern lights. People see similar lights in the sky in Antarctic regions. They are called the *Aurora Australis*, the southern lights. These spectacular shows may happen at the same time because auroras are caused by the sun and the ionosphere of Earth's atmosphere.

When the Italian astronomer Galileo first used a telescope in 1609, he saw black spots moving across the face of the sun. Today, we know that these *sunspots* are huge, violent storms on the sun's surface. Long streams of gas leap from the sun into space during the storms. The gas is made up of tiny particles, and some of them travel to Earth. These gas particles contain electrically charged particles that are magnetic. When the particles are near Earth, they are drawn toward the magnetic poles. The *magnetic poles* are two regions

▼ **An aurora sometimes forms a bright arch of glowing light in the sky. But most auroras are fainter. The most common color for an aurora is green, but displays very high in the sky may be red or purple.**

of the Earth, near the North and South geographic poles, that act like giant magnets. When particles from the sun enter Earth's atmosphere, they sometimes collide with other particles that form Earth's air. These collisions make the glow called aurora.

The more storms there are on the sun, the larger the aurora is. Sometimes the glow can be seen in most of the United States. In 1909, an Aurora Borealis was seen as far south as Singapore, which is almost on the equator! The aurora appears most often in March and April and again in September and October.

▶ ▶ ▶ ▶ **FIND OUT MORE** ◀ ◀ ◀ ◀
Atmosphere; Earth; Radiation Belt; Sun

AUSTEN, JANE (1775–1817)

Jane Austen began writing to amuse herself and her family when she was just a child. She spelled the title of her first book *Love and Freindship*, but her writing and spelling improved as she grew older. Years later, she wrote *Pride and Prejudice*, one of the best-known novels ever written.

Jane Austen, daughter of a minister, was born in Hampshire, England. She was the youngest in a family of seven children and she never married. Life in the small English towns where her father preached could have been dull, but not to Jane. She was interested in everything and everybody. She often used people she knew as models for the characters in her books. This is one reason her stories seem very real and lifelike. Her books are shrewdly observed "comedies of manners," written about the daily lives of real people.

Jane Austen wrote six novels. The first one published was *Sense and Sensibility*. This book and three others: *Pride and Prejudice, Mansfield Park*, and *Emma* were published during her lifetime but without

her name being mentioned, because it was not considered respectable for women to write books. Two more: *Northanger Abbey* and *Persuasion* were published after she died, with her name on them.

AUSTRALIA

Australia is a land that is different from any other place on Earth. Some trees look like bottles. Animal life there is unlike any other in the world: One bird, the emu, cannot fly. Animals, such as the Tasmanian devil and kangaroo, carry their young in a pouch on their abdomen. Even the names of the towns can be unusual, such as Nowhere Else, Come-by-Chance, or Woolloomooloo.

Australia is the smallest continent and the only continent that is also a single country. Australia's nickname is the "Land Down Under." Find Australia on a globe or world map and see if you can explain why it has this nickname.

The Land
Australia is as large as the United States, not counting Alaska and Hawaii. It is a land of low mountains, beautiful beaches, and a dry, nearly empty interior known as *the outback*. Most people live along the eastern and southern coasts, where

▲ Jane Austen, novelist and observer of English society.

▼ Australia's massive sandstone mountain, Ayers Rock, stands in the middle of a desert. It is a sacred aborigine site.

AUSTRALIA

Capital city
Canberra (289,000 people)

Area
2,967,909 square miles
(7,686,848 sq. km)

Highest point
Mount Kosciusko
7,316 feet (2,230 m)

Lowest point
Lake Eyre 52 feet (16 m)
below sea level

Longest river
Murray River 1,609 miles
(2,589 km)

Largest city
Sydney (3,531,000 people)

Population
16,000,000 people

Government
Federal constitutional
monarchy

Natural resources
Bauxite, coal, copper, gold,
iron ore, lead, manganese,
oil, opals, silver, tin,
tungsten, zinc

Export products
Wool, metals and metal
ores, coal, grain, dairy
products, and meat

Unit of money
Australian dollar

Official language
English

the climate is comfortable. The east coast is bordered by the Great Dividing Range of mountains. Australia's highest point, Mount Kosciusko 7,316 feet (2,230 m), is in the southern part of the range. Just to the west of the mountains begins the vast outback, where little rain falls and rivers dry up in the blazing sun. This central region is unsettled except for a few widely scattered mining towns and sheep and cattle ranches known as *stations*. The northern part of the continent changes from desert to tropical jungle. The south-central part has a number of big lakes, the largest being salty Lake Eyre. It is the lowest point in Australia at 52 feet (16 m) below sea level. From the lakes west, the desert extends almost to the sea.

The largest coral formation in the world, the Great Barrier Reef, is found off Australia's northeast coast. This beautiful reef extends for more than 1,200 miles (1,900 km). About 600 islands rise from the Coral Sea along the Great Barrier Reef. Heron Island is one of the most interesting. Giant green turtles come to this island once a year to lay their eggs in the warm sand. These turtles grow to as much as 5 feet (1.5 m) across.

Ayers Rock, in the Northern Territory, is the largest rock outcrop in the world. This natural phenomenon is more than 1,000 feet (300 m) high and 1½ miles (2.5 km) long. The distance around it is almost 6 miles (10 km). The aborigines, the first people to settle in Australia, believe Ayers Rock, which they call Uluru, is sacred. Caves in the bottom of the rock are covered with paintings and carvings made by ancestors of today's aborigines.

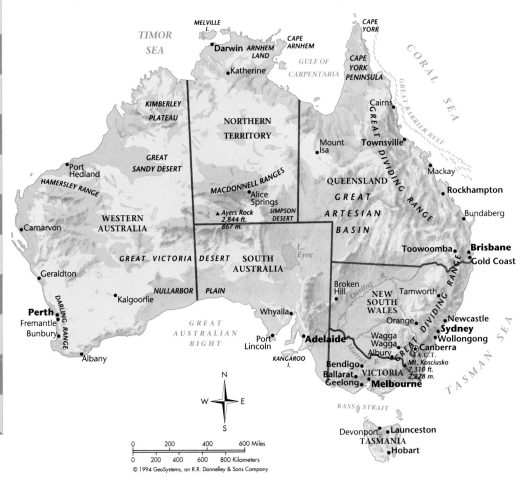

Early History

Aborigines from Southeast Asia migrated to Australia about 45,000 years ago. They lived off the land, hunting and gathering, until the arrival of European settlers destroyed their way of life. Their numbers decreased so rapidly, that today they form only a small percentage of the population.

In the early 1600s, Portuguese, Spanish, and Dutch explorers sighted Australia, but none claimed it until Abel Tasman, a Dutchman, landed in Van Diemen's Land (now called Tasmania) in 1642. The Dutch called the continent New Holland but did not try to settle it.

In 1770, an Englishman, Captain James Cook, landed at what is now Botany Bay. He sailed north along the east coast, claiming it for Britain and calling it New South Wales. But colonization did not start immediately because Britain had to contend with uprisings in the colonies and, later, the Revolutionary War.

The first settlement in Australia came in 1788, at Port Jackson (where Sydney now stands). Of the first 1,500 settlers, 726 were British convicts. Some, including 180 women, were political prisoners. Many were *debtors*—people put in jail because they could not pay their bills. More than 160,000 prisoners had arrived in Australia by the time Great Britain stopped sending convicts in 1868. Among the prisoners were many talented and able people.

Australians, like Americans, had to conquer the wilderness before they could build a permanent nation. Settlers formed six colonies: New South Wales, Tasmania, Western Australia, South Australia, Victoria, and Queensland. Each colony governed itself for many years. The six joined together as states of the Commonwealth of Australia in 1901.

Two territories (the Northern Territory and the Australian Capital Territory) are also part of the nation. The Northern Territory is a huge land mass, part desert and part jungle. Very few people live there. Most work in mines or on remote sheep or cattle stations. The Australian Capital Territory is similar in nature to the District of Columbia in the U.S. Canberra, the national capital of Australia, was built in 1911 on land given by New South Wales. The national government has been established in Canberra since 1927.

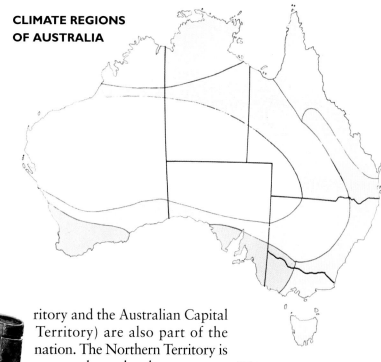

CLIMATE REGIONS OF AUSTRALIA

☐ **Mediterranean**
☐ **Desert**
☐ **Semi-arid**
☐ **Wet and dry tropical**
☐ **Wet subtropical**

◄ **Ned Kelly, the famous Australian outlaw, often wore homemade armor. He was caught and hanged in 1880.**

▼ **Captain Arthur Philip raises the Union Jack at Botany Bay in 1788.**

The Great Barrier Reef is the largest structure ever built by living creatures. It is made of the remains of tiny creatures called *coral polyps*. It extends for about 1,240 miles (2,000 km) off the northeastern coast of Australia (about as long as the west coast of the U.S.A.).

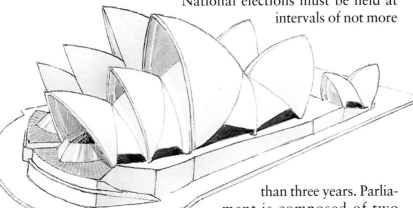

▲ Sydney Opera House was designed to look like billowing sails. Begun in 1959, it was finally finished in 1973.

▼ An Australian sheep station. Wool is the country's chief export product.

Australia Today

Australia is a completely independent nation. It has trade, cultural, and defense links with Britain and the Commonwealth and also has close ties with the United States and with its neighbors in the Pacific and Southeast Asia. The system of government is modeled on the British system. Each state has its own government, but national government rests with the Federal Parliament. National elections must be held at intervals of not more than three years. Parliament is composed of two branches of lawmakers—an upper house called the Senate and a lower house called the House of Representatives. After an election, the leader of the political party or parties that holds a majority of the seats in the House of Representatives is then called upon to form a government composed of Cabinet Ministers. The leader of the ruling party becomes Prime Minister, whose job resembles in many ways that of the U.S. President. Queen Elizabeth II of Great Britain is also Queen of Australia, although she holds no real power. She names a Governor-General to represent her. The real power of the Australian government rests in the hands of the Prime Minister and Parliament.

Two-fifths of Australia's people live in the capital cities of the six states. The capitals and their states are Sydney (New South Wales), Brisbane (Queensland), Melbourne (Victoria), Adelaide (South Australia), Hobart (Tasmania), and Perth (Western Australia).

Until the end of World War II in 1945, almost every new settler in Australia was from England, Scotland, or Ireland. Since the war, however, thousands of immigrants from other European nations and the United States have been admitted. In the 1800s, Australia passed strong laws that prevented immigration by nonwhites from Asia and Africa. This policy of racial discrimination was criticized by many. In 1973, the government relaxed the policy, and since then Indochinese refugees and other Asians have settled in Australia.

Australian Economy

Australia is the world's top wool exporter. One third of all wool used in the world comes from Australia. Sheep stations cover thousands and thousands of acres. Large herds of cattle are raised on Australian cattle stations. Agriculture is very important too. Besides wool, meat, leather, and dairy products, other major agricultural exports are wheat, cereals, sugar, and fruit.

Fish, oysters, and crayfish are important products of the fishing industry. Divers find valuable pearls in the waters off the coasts. Australia is the world's largest producer of mother-of-pearl—a material used to make buttons and decorations.

Gold mining has been important in Australia since the gold rush in 1851. The finest opals in the world are found in Australia. Diamonds, sapphires, and other precious jewels are also mined. Lead, zinc, tin, copper, and other minerals are mined in Australia, along with huge amounts of iron and coal. There are oil fields in Western Australia and also off the coast of Victoria. The country's leading manufactured goods are processed farm products and metals, especially iron and steel.

Wildlife

The continent of Australia split away from the other continents millions of years ago. This means, plants and animals that have disappeared elsewhere still live in Australia, and new species have developed there. About 400 kinds of animals from prehistoric times live on this continent. The kangaroo is the best known of these. The small, cuddly-looking koala is another animal found only in Australia. The duck-billed platypus, an egg-laying mammal with ducklike feet and bill, and the echidna or spiny anteater are descendants of early animals. The dingo is a wild dog that the aborigines probably brought from Asia to Australia many thousands of years ago.

Australian birds are also quite unusual. For example, the kookaburra has a strange call that has earned it the nickname "laughing jackass." The emu is a bird 7 feet (2 m) tall that cannot fly. The cassowary bird cannot fly either, but it can run at speeds of up to 40 miles per hour (64 km/hr). The lyrebird has an unusual tail that is shaped like a feathered harp. The lyrebird can mimic other birds.

Most of Australia's plant life is

Kookaburra

Koala

▲ An aerial view of Sydney, with its famous bridge and opera house. Sydney is the capital of New South Wales.

◄ A kookaburra and a koala, two animal species that are native to the Australian continent.

unlike that of any other continent. Nearly all the trees belong to two groups: acacia and eucalyptus. The acacia grows well in the hot, dry parts of Australia. One acacia species even grows in the desert. The nearly 600 species of eucalyptus grow best in the wetter regions of Australia. But a small species called *mallee* can be found in dry places. Most of Australia has no trees at all—just mile after mile of scrub grass or desert.

Australian Culture

Every Australian child must attend school until he or she is 15 or 16. Government trade schools and agricultural colleges are free. Scholarships help students go to college. Some Australian children learn lessons over two-way radios. This *School of the Air* is for children who live too far from towns and cities to

---

QUIZ

1. As you go south from Darwin to Melbourne, does the temperature get hotter or colder?
2. What does the word *aborigine* mean?
3. Canberra is Australia's capital—but what is its largest city (in population)?
4. Name three of Australia's important agricultural exports.
5. Are koalas marsupials (that is, do they carry their young in a pouch)?

(Answers on page 384)

▲ An Australian aborigine family enjoying a meal together. Aborigines make up about 1 percent of the population of Australia.

▼ The Red kangaroo is the largest of Australia's native mammals. A baby kangaroo is called a joey and it lives in its mother's pouch.

attend regular school. These boys and girls live on lonely cattle and sheep stations in the outback or in mining camps.

Australia is famous for its athletes. Many great tennis and swimming champions have been Australians. Surfers from Australia are famous wherever the sport is popular. Some of the world's best surf is found along Australian coasts. Australian sailing crews have proved their yacht-racing skills by winning the famed America's Cup. Few people know that Australia has more snow-covered areas than Switzerland. (Australia had the world's first ski club, formed in 1860.) The skiing in the Snowy Mountains compares favorably with skiing in the Alps or the Rockies. Many favorite sports, such as cricket, curling, rugby football, and lawn bowling, have come to Australia from Great Britain.

The aboriginal people of Australia had a highly developed artistic tradition long before Europeans arrived. Today their elaborate designs painted on bark and rock are admired all over the world. Despite its remoteness, Australia also has a lively Western culture. Art, music, opera, and ballet are all enthusiastically followed. One

of the world's great opera houses can be found in Sydney. The Australian motion picture industry produces a number of films each year and has received international acclaim.

Australia is divided into two areas. The first area covers the big and small cities. Here 8 out of 10 Australians live among modern buildings and the hustle and bustle common to large population centers elsewhere in the world. But few people live in the interior of the continent, the other area called the *outback*. Some of Australia's 160,000 aborigines still try to follow their traditional life there. Most aborigines have moved to the cities, where they have lost touch with the culture of their ancestors and, at the same time, have found it difficult to become accepted in white society. But campaigns among aboriginal people in the cities, and government projects to protect aboriginal culture, have revived interest in traditonal ways of life. Also the ownership of sacred sites (such as Ayers Rock, in 1985) is being returned to them.

▶ ▶ ▶ ▶ **FIND OUT MORE** ◀ ◀ ◀ ◀
Animals see Australian Mammals; Flightless Birds; Kangaroo; Koala; Mammal; Marsupial; Platypus; Sheep; Spiny Anteater; Whales and Whaling
Explorers see Cook, Captain James
International Relations see Colony; Immigration
People see Aborigine
Topography see Great Barrier Reef; Lake; Murray-Darling Rivers

AUSTRALIAN MAMMALS

Australia has mammals that are found nowhere else on earth. Most of Australia's mammals are *marsupials*, or pouched mammals. Such mammals give birth to young that need to live for weeks or even months in their mother's pouch until they have grown enough to get along

on their own. Most of the world's mammals give birth to young already well developed so they can live safely outside their mother's body. They are called *placental mammals* because the female grows an organ called the placenta. It is a network of tissue that helps send food and oxygen from the mother to the growing baby. The placenta forms when the baby starts to develop in the mother.

The pouched mammals probably *evolved*, or developed, before placental mammals. In most places, the placental animals became powerful enough to take over, and most of the marsupials died out. However, Australia was cut off by sea from other lands before placental mammals reached there. *Kangaroos, koalas, wombats*, and other pouched mammals were free to develop in Australia without having to compete with the more advanced placental mammals.

Every animal on Earth has a special place and way of life called a *niche*. On different continents, the same niche can be occupied by different animals. Marsupials hold almost every niche in Australia that placental mammals hold on other continents. Placental mammals and marsupials that hold the same niche on different continents may even look alike.

In Australia, marsupial rats, mice, cats, and moles occupy niches that placental mammals hold in other parts of the world. Kangaroos hold the grassland niches of grazing animals, such as deer and antelope. Small marsupials called *phalangers*, including the koala, hold the tree-living

niches of squirrels. The roly-poly wombat has teeth and a way of life like that of large placental rodents.

Two other Australian mammals, the *echidna*, or spiny anteater, and the *platypus*, are also very unusual. These two mammals are more closely related to reptiles than any other living mammals. Some of their body parts—the structure of the eye and the shape of the skeleton—are more reptilian than mammalian. More important, these two mammals lay eggs like reptiles but suckle their young like mammals. The young develop and hatch outside the body of the mother. They are the only mammals that hatch their young from eggs.

Marsupials can also be found in the Americas. In South America some niches were never taken over by placental mammals. Therefore, the pouched mammals that filled them were free to continue their way of life. The *opossum*, which eventually moved into North America, is one of these. Such animals are often called *living fossils* because they have changed very little in millions of years.

▶ ▶ ▶ ▶ **FIND OUT MORE** ◀ ◀ ◀ ◀
Australia; Earth History; Evolution; Kangaroo; Koala; Mammal; Marsupial; Platypus; Spiny Anteater

◀ **The platypus is one of Australia's strangest animals. It has a bill like a duck and a body like a beaver, and it lays eggs like a snake.**

▲ **The numbat is one of Australia's rarest animals. Special efforts are being made to protect its habitat in southwest Australia. It feeds on termites, which it finds with its keen sense of smell.**

▼ **The wombat is a burrowing marsupial of southern Australia. The female's pouch conveniently faces backward and therefore is kept clean while it digs its burrow.**

AUSTRIA

Capital city
Vienna (1,483,000 people)

Area
32,374 square miles
(83,849 sq. km)

Population
7,614,000 people

Government
Constitutional republic

Natural resources
Graphite, iron ore, lead,
zinc, timber, hydroelectricity

Export products
Machinery and transport
equipment, chemicals, iron
and steel

Unit of money
Schilling

Official language
German

AUSTRIA

Austria was for hundreds of years the center of a powerful empire that controlled many other European regions. Today, it is a small country about the size of Indiana, in central Europe. Austria is known for its lovely cities, excellent ski resorts, and gracious people. The beautiful Alps extend through Austria from west to east. In the eastern part of the country the Alps open into the Danube Valley, site of the capital city, Vienna. This valley stretches out into a great plain shared by Austria, The Czech Republic, Slovakia, and Hungary. The river Danube, which flows past Vienna, has long been the main travel route between central and eastern Europe.

One-fourth of all Austrians live in Vienna. This city has many trees and parks and narrow, curving streets. Vienna is known the world over for its music. The city is the home of the

of Christ. Charlemagne, 800 years later, won control of what is now Austria from the local rulers. The Hapsburgs, a very powerful family in Europe, ruled Austria for 700 years until 1918. Under the Hapsburgs, Austria ruled one of the most powerful empires in the world, the Austro-Hungarian Empire.

Two world wars ended Austrian power, but Austria has made a comeback and its people live a comfortable life. Austria has a bicameral legislature and a president who is elected for six years.

The country has much industry. Large waterpower plants produce enough electricity for all of Austria and for export to Italy and Switzerland. Important products are iron and steel, aluminum, machine tools, chemicals, textiles, leather, wood, milk, butter, and cheese.

More than half of Austria's trade is

© 1994 GeoSystems, an R.R. Donnelley & Sons Company

famous Vienna Boys Choir, and music lovers from all over the world travel every year to music festivals in Vienna, Salzburg, and Innsbruck.

Several Austrian cities began as Roman army camps, built at the time

with the West. It is not a member of the European Community and is generally neutral in international affairs.

▶▶▶▶ **FIND OUT MORE** ◀◀◀◀
Alps Mountains; Charlemagne;
Danube River; Europe; Hungary;
Strauss, Johann; World War I;
World War II

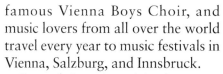

◀ **Austria's picturesque alpine scenery attracts many visitors. In winter, mountain villages are busy ski resorts.**

AUTOGRAPH

An *autograph* is popularly understood to mean a person's *signature,* the name of a person written by himself or herself. The word autograph comes from a Greek word meaning "self-written." An autograph (also called a *holograph*) is actually anything handwritten by a person—a school paper or a shopping list.

The more famous the person, the more valuable his or her writing is likely to be. Also, the value is high if there are very few examples of an autograph and lots of people want to buy it. Items signed by President William Henry Harrison will most likely be worth more than those signed by President Franklin Delano Roosevelt.

AUTOMATION

Automation seems to be a very complicated process. But really it is just a way of having machines do work without human operators controlling the machines every moment they are running. In other words, an *automated* system is a system that works by itself. Every automated system has two parts: (1) a machine (or many machines) that does the work, and (2) another machine that *controls* the first one.

One automated system in the home is a dishwasher. Inside the cabinet is a machine that washes the dishes, rinses them, and dries them. Also inside the cabinet is a device that tells the machine what to do and when to do it. The machine obeys the set of instructions. What good would it do if the machine dried the dishes *before* it washed them?

Your refrigerator is another kind of automated system. Inside is a machine that cools the food. This cooler is controlled by a device that checks the temperature inside the refrigerator. If the food is not cold

The autographs of two famous men from American history.

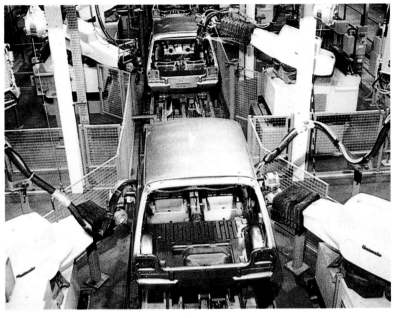

▲ In an automated factory, robot machines do repetitive work, such as welding car bodies.

enough, it automatically switches on the cooler.

Some automated systems, like those that make automobiles, have robots that are controlled by computers. Automated robot systems are able to perform many different kinds of actions and can easily change from one job to another.

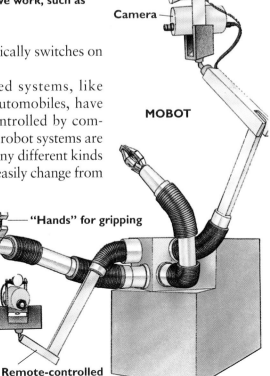

Camera

MOBOT

"Hands" for gripping

▶ This very simple robot, called a "mobot," is used in automation. It has flexible arms for lifting and moving dangerous substances.

Remote-controlled arms

Some kinds of work cannot yet be done by machines. Jobs in which new problems happen frequently, or in which the same actions are not often repeated, are not good candidates for automation. No one has yet built a machine that replaces the work of a doctor. But other jobs, especially repetitive tasks such as calculating sums of money and working on a factory assembly line, can easily be automated.

Automated systems often help people, because machines do work that is boring or even dangerous for people. Jobs such as handling radioactive materials used in nuclear power plants are often done by machines. Automation permits fewer people to manufacture more and better goods, which often means that prices can be lowered.

Automation can also cause big problems. When an automatic system is installed in an office or factory, many workers may lose their jobs. These workers may get special training, however, to learn new jobs.

▶ ▶ ▶ **FIND OUT MORE** ◀ ◀ ◀
Computer; Industrial Revolution;
Manufacturing; Robot

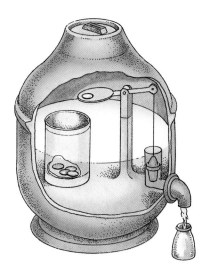

▲ The earliest automation that we know of was invented by Hero of Alexandria in Egypt in the 1st century A.D. He invented a coin-operated machine for selling holy water at a Greek temple. A falling coin triggered a mechanism to release a measure of water into a container.

⚙ AUTOMOBILE

One invention has done more to change the Western world than anything else in the last hundred years. That invention is the automobile.

The automobile is the main reason why our cities are so huge today.

When the centers of cities became too crowded, the automobile took people to the suburbs, but it helped them make the daily trip to jobs in the city. In automobile factories and used-car lots, in oil fields, steel mills, and gas stations, in highway construction and parking garages, thousands of men and women earn their living from the automobile.

But the automobile has also caused problems. Traffic jams delay people. Exhaust fumes add to air pollution. Accidents cause injury and death. In ugly junkyards, old auto bodies pile up. The automobile is a long way from being a perfect means of transportation.

Development of the Automobile
The first vehicle that used its own power to move was built by Nicolas Cugnot in Paris in 1769. It was a small, three-wheeled tractor with a steam engine. The development of self-propelled vehicles continued in Britain in the early 1800s. Unfortunately, the British Parliament thought automobiles too dangerous and tried to stop their use. Parliament passed a law making 4 miles an hour (6.4 km/hr) the speed limit for steam cars. A man also had to walk in front of a "horseless carriage," carrying a red flag during the day and a red lantern at night. This law caused so many problems that for 30 years people stopped experimenting with the horseless carriage. Parliament did not repeal this law until 1896. By then people in Germany, France, and the United States were busy building and driving automobiles.

The *internal combustion engine* gave automobiles the push they needed to become the fastest-growing industry in the world. This kind of an engine provides power by burning, or exploding, fuel and air inside itself.

Some of today's cars are named for the engineers who first built them. In 1885, Karl Benz of Germany built a three-wheeled car with an internal

▼ Cugnot's steam-powered carriage was meant to pull a heavy cannon. It sputtered along at only 3 miles an hour (4.8 km/hr), but it was the first working automobile.

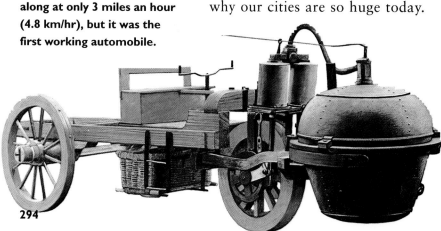

combustion engine. Today the Mercedes-Benz automobile is famous all over the world. Henry Ford built his first car in 1896. He was one of the first people to understand how important automobiles would be. He helped start the Detroit Automobile Company in 1899. By the next year, 8,000 cars were made in the United States. People were getting used to seeing automobiles on the streets. Henry Ford formed the Ford Motor Company in 1903. By that time David Buick also was building automobiles. Another pioneer automaker, Ransom Olds, built a car he called the Oldsmobile.

A few people, however, still preferred steam cars. But they were too heavy and too slow, and steam engines often broke down. Electric cars were popular for a while, but they were not really practical because the batteries would lose power after as little as 30 miles (48 km).

The first automakers built one car at a time, just as carriages had been built. This took a long time and cost a lot of money. It also meant that each car was a little bit different from others because the workers made little changes and improvements on every car. All the people in a factory worked together to build one car. When the first car was finished, they started on the next one.

In 1901, Oldsmobiles were built on the first *assembly line*. On an assembly line, car parts were pushed from worker to worker. Each person did the same job over and over. About 5,000 Oldsmobiles were built in 1903 with this new system.

But Henry Ford was the man who really made the automobile so important to life in America. He introduced the Model T Ford in 1908. He improved the assembly line idea in 1913. To the assembly line, he added *conveyor belts*, moving belts that carried car parts from worker to worker faster than ever before. The new Ford system could build six cars in the time it used to take to build one! And it was cheaper to make them. The Model T Ford cost more than 800 dollars in 1908. It cost only 400 dollars when it was built on the new assembly line in 1916.

Henry Ford knew that in order to make and sell many cars, he would have to produce one model at a price that most people could afford. One way he did this was with the assembly line. Another idea he used to build low-priced cars was *standardization*. This meant that each Model T coming from the factory was exactly the same as every other Model T made that year. This process of manufacturing allowed him to produce many inexpensive cars. He would not even paint Model T's different colors. A popular joke of the time was, "You can get a

AUTOMOBILE FIRSTS

1885 Karl Benz (Germany) builds first automobile

1886 Gottlieb Daimler (Germany) builds first four-wheeled automobile

1895 Pneumatic tires developed by Michelin brothers (France)

1898 First fully enclosed automobile, Renault

1908 Henry Ford introduces Model T

1913 Moving conveyor belt speeds up Ford assembly line

1928 First car with synchromesh gears, Cadillac

1939 First automatic transmission, Oldsmobile

1950 First gas-turbine car, Rover (Britain)

1980 General Motors introduces cars with computers

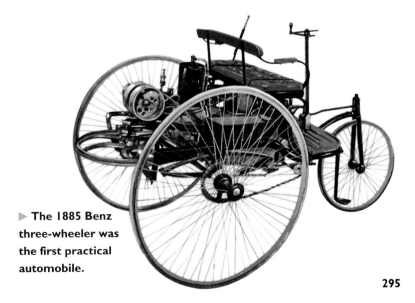

▶ The 1885 Benz three-wheeler was the first practical automobile.

▲ This 1957 Cadillac has typical 1950s body styling, with huge fins and grilles.

▼ A Volkswagen Beetle. First built in the 1930s, it is the biggest selling car of all time.

Moving an Automobile

An automobile is a complicated machine. Several things happen when a driver turns the *ignition key.* The key turns on a switch. This lets electricity flow from the car *battery* to a small electric motor. The motor turns a *crankshaft,* a specially-formed bar over and over. *Rods* connected to the crankshaft go up and down as the shaft turns. The rods force *pistons* up and down inside tubes, or *cylinders.* The key turns on the *ignition* (starting) system at the same time. More electricity flows from the battery. First, the electricity goes into a *coil* that increases its voltage. Then the electricity goes to a *distributor.* The distributor has one *contact,* for each cylinder. A small *rotor* (wheel) spins around and touches each contact many times every second. Each time a contact is touched, electricity flows to that cylinder. Today's cars have an electronic ignition system that distributes the energy to each *spark plug.* A spark plug sticking into the cylinder receives the electricity and gives off a powerful spark. This spark causes a mixture of fuel and air in the cylinder to explode. (Gasoline is the most common fuel. Some engines burn liquid propane. Large diesel engines burn heavier oil similar to kerosene.) The explosion of the fuel and air pushes the piston down. The engine is then running. A small *alternator* now takes over for the battery, to produce electricity as long as the engine runs. The battery is used only to start the engine.

But the car still is not moving—to make it move, power from the engine must turn the wheels. That is the job of the *transmission.* Connecting rods and pistons moving up and down keep the crankshaft spinning. The other end of the crankshaft connects to the transmission, or gearbox. The spinning crankshaft turns a gear. The driver chooses this gear by changing the position of a lever near the

Model T in any color you want, as long as it's black."

Ford was right. His Model T became the best-selling car in the world. Other auto builders took 20 years to catch up with Ford. Americans were driving about 15 million Model T's by the time the Ford factory started building Model A Fords in 1928.

▼ A diagram of a modern automobile showing the main parts. The transmission system carries the turning motion of the engine from the crankshaft to the driving wheels, which are usually at the rear of the automobile.

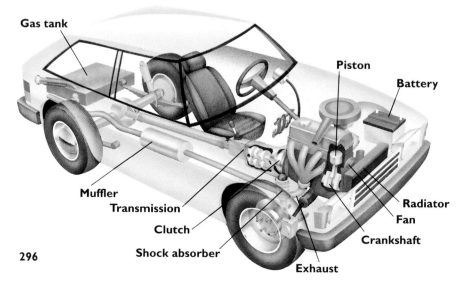

Gas tank

Piston

Battery

Muffler

Transmission

Clutch

Shock absorber

Radiator

Fan

Crankshaft

Exhaust

steering wheel or on the floor. If gear A is twice as big as gear B, then—when they are turning together—B will go twice as fast as A. The gears are mounted on a *driveshaft,* a straight bar connected by gears to one or both of the car's *axles* (usually the rear one). When the driveshaft turns, so does the axle. Since the wheels are attached to the ends of the axle, they must spin when the axle turns. The wheels turn faster or slower each time the driver changes gears. Power from the engine is applied smoothly to the driving wheels by means of the *clutch* (a set of discs that are pressed together) or an *automatic transmission.*

The Automobile Today

A typical automobile in the United States today has more than 5,000 parts. Many companies make only one or two of these parts, then ship them to an automobile assembly plant. Raw materials that go into making a car come from all over the world. And there are automobile plants in many countries. More imported cars are now sold in the United States than ever before.

Today's automobiles come in many different shapes, sizes, and colors. A truck is a kind of automobile, whether it is a giant tractor-trailer truck that hauls loads across the country or a small pickup truck that takes farm products to market. For many years the most popular cars in the United States were large sedans and station wagons that could carry six passengers or more. But the rising cost of gasoline has caused many people to prefer compact cars with smaller engines because they get better mileage than engines in larger cars.

Automobiles cause about half the accidental deaths in the world. So each year automakers try for improvements in car safety. Padded dashboards, collapsible steering posts, seat belts, air bags, and safety bars in doors and roofs are safety equipment that help save lives. Car bodies are made so that in a collision they crumple gradually and absorb much of the force of impact. Improvements in braking systems such as antilock brakes, help drivers to stop quickly in an emergency, without skidding.

The growing numbers of cars and

Modern automobile assembly plants have been made more efficient by the use of robots. These automated machines have taken over many of the repetitive tasks on the production line.

trucks on the roads go on causing traffic jams in busy cities. The exhaust from cars continues to pollute the air. In Los Angeles, automobiles are the main cause of air pollution. Governments around the world are trying to tackle the problems caused by cars. In some countries, automobiles must be fitted with a *catalytic converter,* which reduces the amount of harmful gases blown out with the exhaust. Unleaded gasoline is also less harmful to the environment. Some cities have set up car pooling arrangements, and have banned cars from certain areas.

▶▶▶▶ **FIND OUT MORE** ◀◀◀◀
Air Pollution; Bus; City; Driving; Duryea, Charles and Frank; Engine; Ford, Henry; Trucks and Trucking

WHERE TO DISCOVER MORE

Sutton, Richard. *Car.* New York: Knopf, 1990.
Cole, Joanna. *Cars and How They Go.* New York: Crowell, 1983.

AUTO RACING

Auto racing is an exciting and dangerous sport. Each year millions of spectators line roads and racetracks throughout the world to watch high-powered cars race for fun, fame, and prize money.

There are two main types of auto races—*track races* and *road races.* Track races are run on oval tracks that have straight, flat, high-speed sections, or *straightaways,* and banked or unbanked curves. Road races are run on specially built road courses or on ordinary roads. These courses have sharp curves and hills.

Probably the most famous track race is the Indianapolis 500. It is run each year on Memorial Day weekend at the Indianapolis Motor Speedway. Drivers race at average speeds of more than 200 miles per hour (320 km/hr) around the $2\frac{1}{2}$ mile (4 km) Indy track. The first to complete 200 laps wins the race.

Each year, high-performance racing cars compete in an international series of as many as 16 *Grand Prix* road races, each of which is held in a different country. Every year at least one Grand Prix is held in the United States. Grand Prix cars are known as *Formula One* cars; there are rules governing car design and engine size. Grand Prix races are 150 to 250 miles (240 to 400 km) long. The win-

ner is the first to complete the required number of laps around the course. Points are given to the winner and runners-up. The driver with the most Grand Prix points at the end of the year wins the World Driver's Championship. Other types of cars compete in endurance races, such as the 24-hour races at Daytona, Florida, and at Le Mans, France.

Sports car racing, stock car racing, drag racing, hill climbs, and cross-country rallies are other enjoyable kinds of auto competition. Often the cars are regular production models, specially modified to squeeze the best performance out of them. The Canadian-American (Can-Am) Challenge Cup is a well-known race for high-speed sports cars. Another is the Trans-Am series, run by the Sports Car Club of America. In rally driving, cars are driven fast over rough country roads.

Stock car racing attracts many spectators in the United States and Canada. Drivers in *souped up* or supercharged everyday cars, ranging from *jalopies* (old cars) to the latest models, compete on oval tracks (some on road courses). Stock cars are stripped down for lightness. Steel *roll bars* are usually added to strengthen the inside cage of stock cars. Fuel tanks are small in stock cars. Here, as in other auto races, drivers make quick stops at special areas called *pits*

▼ Race drivers compete for points. At the end of the season, after at least 16 races held at different racetracks, the driver with the most points wins the Indy Car World Series.

to refuel. Tire changes and repairs are also sometimes done during *pitstops*.

Drag racing is also popular in the United States and Canada. Souped up cars *accelerate* (gain speed) from a standing start and race down straightaways. *Draggers* (drag racing cars) have extra-large, wide rear wheels made of soft, sticky rubber to help grip the track. The fastest draggers can travel a quarter mile (402 m) in less than six seconds.

▶ ▶ ▶ ▶ **FIND OUT MORE** ◀ ◀ ◀ ◀
Automobile; Driving

AUTUMN

Autumn is the season of the year that occurs between summer and winter. Americans usually call this season fall, the time when leaves on many trees wither and fall to the ground. The leaves of maple and elm trees turn to red and yellow before they fall, while brown oak leaves often remain on trees throughout the winter. The needle-like leaves of fir trees stay green all year around.

The air in autumn is usually crisp and cool. At night, the harvest moon shines, huge and round. The days grow shorter. In the Northern Hemisphere, autumn begins about September 22, the day known as the *autumnal equinox*. It is one of two days each year when day and night are equal in length. Autumn ends on about December 22, the day of the *winter solstice*. In the Southern Hemisphere, September marks the beginning of spring, not the beginning of autumn.

A period of warm, mild weather often occurs after the first frost in autumn. This is known as *Indian summer* because it feels like summer again.

As winter approaches, many birds fly south. Animals such as squirrels, rabbits, and raccoons store food to eat during the winter. Other animals prepare to *hibernate* (sleep through

the cold months)—bears in caves, bats inside hollow trees, and fish at the bottom of ponds.

▶ ▶ ▶ ▶ **FIND OUT MORE** ◀ ◀ ◀ ◀
Halloween; Leaf; November;
Season; September; Thanksgiving;
Veterans Day

▲ **Autumn is a time of natural beauty. The leaves change color, from green to red, gold, and brown, and leaves cover the ground.**

AVIATION

Have you ever wanted to soar high through the air like a bird? Since earliest times, people have wanted to fly. For thousands of years, they were jealous of birds, which flew swiftly overhead while people struggled to walk through jungles, across deserts, and over snow and ice. The human desire to fly is expressed in ancient myths that tell of winged gods and of heroes who traveled the skies in flying chariots. A Greek myth says that Daedalus and his son, Icarus, flew with bird-like wings made of wax, twine, and the feathers of seabirds. Arabian legends tell of people, such as Aladdin, flying over cities on magic carpets.

▼ **Leonardo da Vinci's idea for a helicopterlike flying machine in the early 1500s.**

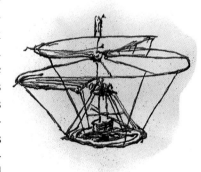

People first tried to learn the secret of flight during the Middle Ages. The first experimenters thought they could imitate birds. They made wings, strapped them to their arms, and leaped from high places, flapping as hard as they could. But the human body was not designed for flapping flight, so these would-be "birdmen"

▲ Leonardo da Vinci's sketch of an ornithopter. He thought it would carry people through the air if they flapped their wings like birds.

crashed to earth. Later inventors designed flying machines called *ornithopters,* which also had wings that could be flapped. But they would not carry a person. A small model ornithopter will fly slowly, in calm air. However, flapping flight was not the answer.

The first truly scientific study of flight was made in the late 1400s by the brilliant Italian artist and inventor, Leonardo da Vinci. Leonardo realized that human arm and chest muscles are not strong enough to work a pair of wings. But he did design some wing devices that could be attached to both the arms and the legs. He also made detailed drawings of ornithopters, helicopters, and parachutes. The notes and sketches he left show that Leonardo had a good understanding of the principles of flight. But historians are not sure whether he ever built and tested his inventions.

The First Flying Machines

The first flying invention to get off the ground was a floating machine, a *balloon.* In 1783 two Frenchmen, the Montgolfier brothers, built a huge balloon and filled it with hot air. Because hot air rises, the balloon was able to leave the ground and then float through the air. The Montgolfiers' balloon drifted 5 miles (8 km) in 25 minutes, with two men seated in a basket attached to it. A balloon filled with hydrogen gas, which is lighter than air, was successfully launched later the same year. These early balloon flights were dangerous and not very practical because the balloonists could not control the direction in which they floated. They had to go wherever the wind took them. During the 1800s, people tried to guide balloons by using propellers and steam engines. But the engines were too heavy and could not produce enough power.

Inventors meanwhile continued to study the use of winged machines. They had come to realize that fixed wings were better than flapping ones. Many of them built *gliders,* planes without engines, with wings held steady by wires. The glider was an important development in the growth of aviation, because it was the first successful heavier-than-air

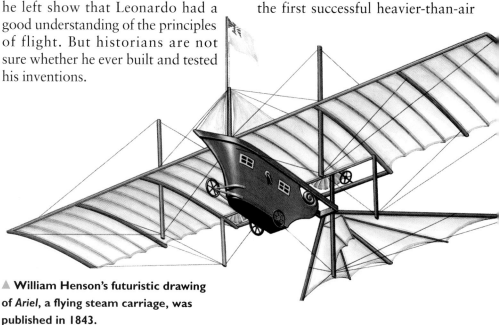

▲ The balloon first took people into the air, beginning with the Montgolfiers' hot-air balloon in 1783.

▲ William Henson's futuristic drawing of *Ariel,* a flying steam carriage, was published in 1843.

craft. Although it could not really fly, it could coast on air for long distances. Its direction could be controlled by moving parts of the wings and tail, and it could be landed safely. Otto Lilienthal of Germany was one of the great pioneers of the glider. He made more than 2,000 flights during the 1890s.

Other inventors tried adding propellers and lightweight engines to their gliders. These were the first airplanes. In 1886, Clement Ader, a French engineer, built a monster of a plane with huge, batlike wings. Driven by a single propeller connected to a steam engine, it flew only a few feet before crashing. Sir Hiram Maxim of England was even less successful. His steam-powered airplane, tested in 1894, barely got off the ground. An American, Samuel Langley, seemed to be on the right track with his *aerodrome* meaning "air runner." But he never got a chance to perfect his plane because he ran out of money.

Two American brothers, Orville and Wilbur Wright, finally came up with the best aircraft of all. They had built and tested many gliders, using different wing designs. They then added a gasoline engine and propellers. Orville piloted the plane on its first successful flight in 1903, at Kitty Hawk, North Carolina. The ancient dream of joining the birds in flight had come true.

Airplanes were soon being built in Europe. France, England, Germany, and Italy made their own models. New designs were tried out to make airplanes more practical, but the early models were still too dangerous to be used for transportation or commerce. Instead, they were used for entertainment and races. Airplanes were new and exciting, and people were happy to pay to see them perform. The first international exhibition was held in Rheims, France, in 1909. Many prizes were offered for the best airplanes and the most skill-

ful pilots. The backers of the exhibition expected about 50,000 people. But more than 250,000 people attended. The success of this and other air meets led airplane makers to build better models in order to win more prizes and attract bigger crowds.

Daredevil pilots called *barnstormers* traveled all over the United States to perform thrilling stunts at carnivals and county fairs. They raced with automobiles and other airplanes. They walked on the wing of a plane in flight or hung by their hands or knees from the landing gear. They picked up handkerchiefs off the ground with a hook on the tip of the wing. Sometimes they dropped candy and flowers to the cheering crowd below. Some of the more daring members of the audience would pay for a private ride after the show. Barnstormers were often paid a great deal of money for their amazing stunts. They led dangerous lives, and many were killed. But they helped to introduce aviation to the American public.

The airplane became a weapon of war when World War I started in

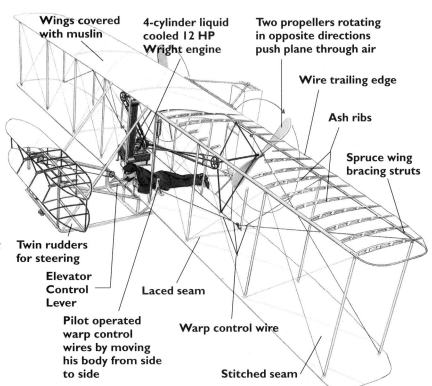

Wings covered with muslin · 4-cylinder liquid cooled 12 HP Wright engine · Two propellers rotating in opposite directions push plane through air · Wire trailing edge · Ash ribs · Spruce wing bracing struts · Twin rudders for steering · Elevator Control Lever · Laced seam · Pilot operated warp control wires by moving his body from side to side · Warp control wire · Stitched seam

▲ The original Wright brothers' flying-machine, *Flyer.* Its first four successful flights were made on December 17, 1903.

Spad XII (French)

Fokker D VIII (German)

Bristol Fighter (British)

▲ World War I speeded up the development of the airplane. The Fokker was a German fighter plane. The other two were Allied planes.

1914. The warring nations of Europe wanted as many planes as they could get, to use for observation, bombing, and other purposes. Small companies that had been building planes slowly, by hand, began to speed up production. They hired the best scientists and engineers.

Modern Aviation

Since World War I, rapid progress has been made in aviation. Regular airmail service between New York and Washington began in 1918. Coast-to-coast service was first offered in 1924. Spectacular record-making flights—such as Charles Lindbergh's solo crossing of the Atlantic Ocean in 1927—proved the power, speed, and safety of the airplane. During the 1930s, commercial airlines began carrying passengers and cargo in Europe and America. Airplanes had become an important means of transport. The first practical helicopter was also developed at this time.

World War II brought even greater advances in aviation, with the coming of the jet age—though only a few jet planes were flown in action. Operational jet aircraft had been developed by the end of the war, in Germany, Great Britain, and the United States. By the late 1950s airlines were using jet airliners, such as the Boeing 707. More and more

people took to the air, and holiday travel by air became big business worldwide.

The 1970s saw the introduction of the world's first commercial faster-than-sound airliner, the Concorde. And the 1980s brought a new kind of aircraft, the Space Shuttle. The Shuttle can fly like a spacecraft in space, but glide back to land on the ground, like a plane. The latest airliners are much quieter and use less fuel than older types. The most recent military *Stealth* aircraft are designed to be almost invisible to radar.

The aviation, or aerospace, industry is the second largest in the United States (after automobile making). Aircraft have many uses, and there are many different types—from the small, slow planes used for crop dusting to the supersonic jets of the Air Force. The Boeing 747 jumbo jet is so big that the Boeing Company built the world's largest building outside Seattle, Washington, as a factory for making the huge planes. Millions of people are employed in the aerospace industry.

▶▶▶▶ **FIND OUT MORE** ◀◀◀◀
Air Force; Airline; Airplane; Airship; Balloon; Glider; Helicopters; Jet Propulsion; Lindbergh, Charles; Wright Brothers

▼ A U.S. Army Apache helicopter. Helicopters were first designed in Germany in the 1930s. They are the only aircraft that can hover at any height. They have been widely used by the military since the Korean War (1950–1953).

▶ How aircraft speeds increased after World War II. The speed of sound, or Mach I, is 760 mph (1,223 km/hr) at sea level. Higher up, sound travels more slowly. So at 36,000 feet (11,000m) Mach I is only 660 mph (1,062 km/hr).

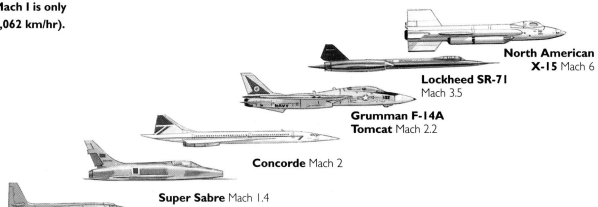

North American X-15 Mach 6

Lockheed SR-71 Mach 3.5

Grumman F-14A Tomcat Mach 2.2

Concorde Mach 2

Super Sabre Mach 1.4

Bell X-1 Mach 1

Spitfire 400 mph

AZERBAIJAN

Azerbaijan is a land of mountains, dry plateaus, and fertile coastal lowlands. It lies in the Caucasus region of southeast Europe. Its eastern border is the Caspian Sea. Azerbaijan is bordered by Russia and Georgia to the north, Armenia to the west, and Iran and Turkey to the south. It is part of the Commonwealth of Independent States, a group of countries that had been part of the U.S.S.R. until 1991.

Oil is the chief natural resource and the principal export of Azerbaijan. The main oil fields are in the area around the capital, Baku, which is a port on the Caspian Sea. Other important wells are located just offshore. Refineries in Baku turn the crude oil into a number of other products, such as gasoline, synthetic rubber, and plastics. Other Baku factories can the products of the Caspian Sea fishing fleet. Caviar, or the eggs of the sturgeon, is a delicacy that is sold around the world.

Farming is also an important source of income. Central Azerbaijan and the coastal lowlands have fertile lands and a warm climate that is sometimes called mediterranean. Mild winters and hot, sunny summers allow farmers to grow cotton, tobacco, tea, rice and citrus fruits. Under Soviet rule, most of these crops were grown on collective farms, where families pooled their crops so that they could be sold together. Since early 1992, farmers have been able to operate independently on their own farms.

Most of northern Azerbaijan lies in the Caucasus Mountains, where the colder climate and poorer soil are better suited to grazing livestock. Fewer people live in this region or in the rugged western plateau.

Azerbaijan takes its name from the Azerbaijani, a Muslim people who speak a language like Turkish. These people make up the majority of the population of Azerbaijan. Millions more Muslims live across the border in neighboring Iran.

About a tenth of the population of Azerbaijan is Armenian. These people are Christian and have little in common with the Azerbaijanis. Most of the Armenians live in Nagorno-Karabakh, a region of Azerbaijan where they form the majority.

Nagorno-Karabakh has been the scene of fierce fighting between the Armenians and the Azerbaijanis. Many Armenians living there want the region to become part of Armenia. The two sides fought several skirmishes in 1989 over this issue. Soviet troops arrived in 1990 to end this civil war. The Soviet government decided that Nagorno-Karabakh should remain part of Azerbaijan.

Now that Azerbaijan and Armenia are no longer governed from Moscow, it remains to be seen whether they can resolve their differences.

▶ ▶ ▶ ▶ **FIND OUT MORE** ◀ ◀ ◀ ◀
Armenia; Russian History

AZERBAIJAN

Capital city
Baku (1,700,000)

Area
33,591 square miles
(87,000 sq. km)

Population
7,030,000

Government
Republic

Natural resources
Oil, minerals, including coal, cobalt, iron ore, aluminum ore, copper

Export products
Oil and oil-related products, iron, steel, cement, chemical products, caviar, fish

Official Language
Russian and Armenian

Unit of Money
Ruble

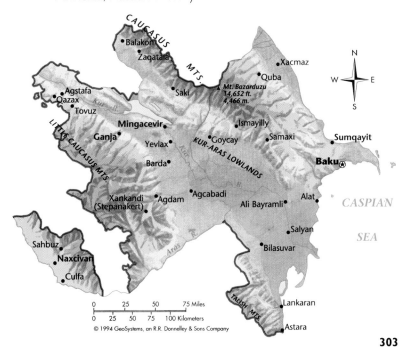

© 1994 GeoSystems, an R.R. Donnelley & Sons Company

AZTECS

▶ Quetzalcoatl, the plumed serpent, was one of the chief Aztec gods. He was worshiped for having brought civilization and education to the Aztecs.

▼ The Aztecs grew many different kinds of fruit. The fruits pictured below were not known in Europe until they were taken there by explorers during the 16th century.

Avocado

Tomato

Lime

▶ Members of the Aztec royal family were carried around on litters, even when they were traveling by boat. No one was allowed to look at the emperor, and if they did, they were risking death.

Legends say that the Aztecs came from northern Mexico. In 1168, on the instructions of their god Huit-zilopochtli, they began to migrate. They eventually settled in the valley of Mexico. In 1325 the Aztecs started to build a city, Tenochtitlán, on an island in Lake Texcoco, which is now the site of Mexico City. In the fifteenth century they went on to conquer the other cities in the valley and founded the Aztec empire. Tenochtitlán was the capital of this empire and was estimated to have had a population of 150,000 people. In order to feed all these people the Aztecs dug canals and drained marshes to make farmland. They also heaped mud into huge, woven-reed baskets and sank the baskets to the bottom of shallow lakes to make artificial islands, or *chinampas*. They planted trees on these islands, and

the trees took root in the bottom of the lakes. In time, the islands became farmlands.

Corn was the main crop of the Aztecs. The women made a coarse cornmeal by grinding corn between two stones. They made flat cakes, called *tortillas*, out of this coarse meal. The Aztecs also grew avocados, limes, beans, chili peppers, cotton, squash, tomatoes, and tobacco. They hunted birds and fish and bred turkeys.

The Aztecs built their houses out of mud and twigs that they wove together. They thatched the roofs with grass. Canals ran between farms and continued into the city. Up and down the canals, people in dug-out canoes hauled their produce to market. Tenochtitlán became a splendid city, with gardens and a zoo.

The Aztecs were skillful stone carvers and artists. They loved jewels and decorated pottery. People who had been conquered by the Aztecs brought gold, silver, and jade for the Aztec craftsmen. Brightly colored

feathers were used to make decorated capes, fans, shields, and headdresses.

Religion was very important to the Aztecs. They depended on forces of nature—the sun, rain, and wind—to help them grow crops, so the Aztecs worshiped these forces as gods. They believed that "good gods," such as the sun god, had to be kept strong. The good gods could prevent certain bad gods from taking control and ruining the lives of the people. They believed that one way they could keep a good god strong was to feed him human hearts and blood. Each year Aztec priests sacrificed many men and women to the gods. One year, about 50,000 prisoners of war were killed. These human sacrifices were carried out at the top of huge, pyramid-shaped temples in an enormous square that stood right in the middle of the city of Tenochtitlán.

Hernando Cortés, a Spanish explorer, led more than 500 Spaniards into Mexico to search for gold in 1519. At first the Aztecs believed Cortés was the representative of a white-skinned god, so they respected him. Then he angered them by melting down their gold ornaments and shipping the gold to Spain. A young Aztec named Cuauhtemoc led the people against the Spaniards, who were forced to retreat. Cuauhtemoc became emperor of the Aztecs when his uncle, Emperor Montezuma, was killed by the Spaniards in 1520. Cuauhtemoc again led his people when Cortés and his men returned to attack Tenochtitlán. But the Aztecs' war clubs could not overcome the Spaniards' muskets. The Spaniards killed the young emperor and completely destroyed the capital city in 1521. The Spaniards built Mexico City on its ruins.

▶▶▶▶ **FIND OUT MORE** ◀◀◀◀
Cortés, Hernando; Native American Art; Native Americans; Mexico; Mexico City

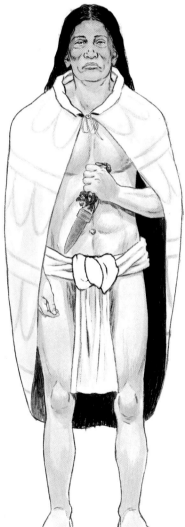

▲ **When Cortés and his men arrived in Tenochtitlán, the Aztecs thought that they were all gods. Emperor Montezuma showered them with gifts.**

◀ **Priests were a very special class of people in Aztec society. They were responsible for making the human sacrifices to keep the gods happy.**

WHERE TO DISCOVER MORE

Beck, Barbara L. *The Aztecs.* New York: Franklin Watts, 1983.
Fisher, Leonard Everett. *Pyramid of the Sun, Pyramid of the Moon.* New York: Macmillan, 1988.

The Semitic B
c. 1500 BC

The
Phoenician B
c. 1000 BC

The Greek B
c. 600 BC

The Roman B
c. AD 600

BABBAGE, CHARLES (1792–1871)

It often seemed to Charles Babbage that his life was nothing but a complete failure, but today he is regarded as a genius. He was a British inventor and mathematician, and one of his inventions was the first modern computer, which he called an "analytical engine." Babbage had the idea for this in 1834. But his computer was never completed. It would not have worked even if it had been, because its levers and gears could not be made accurately at that time. However, in planning it, Babbage worked out many of the principles of modern computers. He planned to use punched cards to feed in information and instructions, and he worked out ways for the machine to store the results of sums in its memory so that those results could later be used to solve more complicated sums. Babbage's partially completed "analytical engine" is in London's Science Museum today.

In 1847, Babbage invented an *ophthalmoscope*, a device to let doc-

▲ Charles Babbage, a computing pioneer.

tors look at the retinas of patients' eyes, but the doctor to whom he lent his model for testing forgot all about it! A few years later a German named Hermann von Helmholtz invented a similar device, which was a success. Near the end of his life Babbage tried to invent a way to place winning bets on horse races, but again he was unsuccessful.

▶▶▶▶ **FIND OUT MORE** ◀◀◀◀
Computer

BABYLONIA

The Babylonians lived thousands of years ago in the ancient land of Mesopotamia, now called Iraq. But the first civilized people to live there, around 6,000 years ago, were Sumerians. Sumer was conquered by Akkadians over 4,000 years ago, and the land was called Sumer and Akkad. Later on, about 1720 B.C., a Babylonian king named Hammurabi conquered other kingdoms around Babylonia and built an empire. He ruled well, but his empire weakened and was taken over by Assyria. Then another king, Nebuchadnezzar, defeated the Assyrians and started another strong empire. He also made Babylon his capital city and built many magnificent temples there.

The Babylonians were good farm-

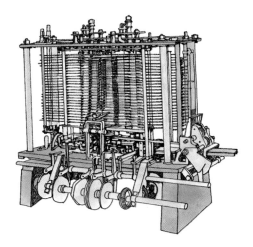

▼ A model of Babbage's "Analytical Engine," a mechanical calculating machine.

▲ The black line on this map shows the extent of the Babylonian empire under Hammurabi the Great and his successors. Hammurabi was a highly efficient ruler.

ers with fine *irrigation,* or watering, systems, an idea they borrowed from the Sumerians. They knew about surveying land, engineering, astronomy, medicine, and astrology. They used the 60-minute hour and the 24-hour day to tell time. Two of their most famous stories are the *Creation Story* that tells about the world's creation by Marduk, the sun god of Babylon, and the *Gilgamesh epic* that describes a flood similar to that in the Bible. *The Code of Hammurabi* was a system of law handed down from King Hammurabi that covered every part of daily life. In the city of Babylon were the famous *Hanging Gardens,* one of the Seven Wonders of the Ancient World, and many pyramid-shaped towers called *ziggurats.* One of them may have been the *Tower of Babel* described in the Bible.

The Babylonians believed that there were as many as 4,000 gods. Everyone had his or her own personal god. People lived by the rules of justice, law and order, courage, kindness, and truth. In 539 B.C., the country was taken over by the Persian Empire, and then conquered by Alexander the Great. Babylonia never again regained its independence or its lost glories. The site of the ruins of ancient Babylonia still exist in modern Iraq.

▶▶▶▶ **FIND OUT MORE** ◀◀◀◀
Ancient Civilizations; Assyria; Mesopotamia; Seven Wonders of the World; Sumer; Time

▲ A statue of Ishtar, a mother-goddess to the Babylonians. To other peoples, such as the Assyrians, Ishtar was the goddess of war.

◀ The Ishtar Gate (named after the goddess Ishtar) was the northern entrance to Babylon. It was covered with blue glazed tiles, which were decorated with yellow and white figures of bulls and dragons.

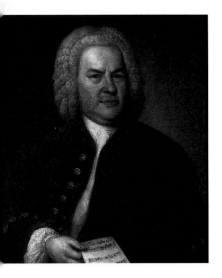

The beginning of the first of six concertos that Bach dedicated to the Margrave of Brandenburg in 1721.

Johann Sebastian Bach, the most famous member of a family of musicians.

Sir Francis Bacon, English statesman and philosopher.

BACH FAMILY

Many fine musicians came from the talented Bach family of Germany. At least 50 Bach family members were musicians in the 17th and 18th centuries. One of them, Johann Sebastian, was one of the greatest composers of all time.

The first member of the family whom we know about was Veit Bach, a baker who died in 1619. Veit liked music, and his son, Hans, was a fiddle player. All of Hans's sons became musicians. Soon, many Bachs were musicians in churches and in the courts of noblemen. If one died or moved away, an uncle or cousin often replaced him.

Johann Sebastian Bach (1685–1750) was born in Eisenach, Germany. His father was Johann Ambrosius, great-grandson of Veit. Johann's parents died when he was 10 years old, and he lived with his older brother. During this time Johann learned to play the harpsichord. He won a scholarship as a choirboy when he was 15, and he studied voice and organ music. He held several teaching positions and then moved to Leipzig, Germany, in 1723, where he stayed until his death. Bach worked as a teacher, organist, and music director at St. Thomas's School and Church.

Bach wrote music all during his life, but almost none of it was performed while he was alive. He won honor as a musician, but not until long after he died did the world acclaim him as a great composer. For almost 100 years, musical interest took a turn away from the kind of music he had written. Bach's works for chorus and orchestra include *The Passion According to St. John, The Passion According to St. Matthew, the Christmas Oratorio*, and the *Mass in B Minor*. He also wrote hundreds of other pieces for keyboard, organ, and orchestra. Many of them are in the embellished style called *Baroque,* with different melodic lines going on at the same time, and passages in which musicians were encouraged to ornament the melody with trills and other notes they might improvise.

Bach married his cousin, Maria, in 1707. They had seven children before she died in 1720. Bach married Anna Wilcken the next year, and they had 13 children together. Two of Bach's sons, Carl Philip Emanuel (1714–1788) and Johann Christian (1735–1782), were also famous composers.

▶▶▶▶ **FIND OUT MORE** ◀◀◀◀
Baroque Period; Choral Music; Composer; Music; Organ

BACON, FRANCIS (1561–1626)

Francis Bacon was an important English statesman and philosopher. He was born in London and went to Trinity College in Cambridge. He served King James I as Attorney General, as Lord Chancellor, and as chief minister of state. Bacon often gave very good advice to King James, who knighted him. But while Bacon was Lord Chancellor, he was found guilty of taking a bribe—accepting money for a dishonest favor. He was sent to the prison in the Tower of London. The king finally let him out of jail, and Bacon spent the rest of his life writing.

He often wrote about honesty, truth, love, and friendship. His greatest contribution was in writing about the scientific method. He helped improve science by telling scientists to observe—to study carefully—the things they wanted to explain. Some people think that Bacon wrote the plays of Shakespeare, but most experts disagree. The books and essays that Bacon did write are still read by people all over the world.

▶▶▶▶ **FIND OUT MORE** ◀◀◀◀
Science

BACON, ROGER
(about 1220–1292)

Roger Bacon was a medieval scientist and experimenter. He was extremely clever and because of this he was accused of being a magician.

Bacon was born in Ilchester, England, and studied at Oxford Univer-

sity. He taught in Paris for a time and returned to Oxford about 1251. He took up a broad study of languages, mathematics, logic, and science—including astronomy, alchemy, and optics (the study of light and vision). About 1257, Bacon became a Franciscan monk, and some of his ideas got him into trouble with the other monks.

Pope Clement IV heard of Bacon's

ideas and secretly asked him to write a book on the sciences. Bacon wrote *Opus Majus* or "Great Work," an encyclopedia of the scientific knowledge of his day. He was later put in jail for a time but managed to write two more scientific books.

Bacon was the first known European to write about gunpowder. He predicted automobiles, submarines, frozen foods, balloons, and a sort of airplane with flapping wings. Most important was his belief that people can learn more from experience and reason than from merely following old ideas. He taught others to gain knowledge by experiment and not to accept old beliefs without question.

▶▶▶▶ **FIND OUT MORE** ◀◀◀◀
Alchemy; Astronomy; Science

BACTERIA

Bacteria live in air, in water, in soil, in most food and drink, and in the bodies of animals and plants. Bacteria (the singular is *bacterium*) are tiny single-celled organisms. Some bacteria can move about, so scientists once thought they were animals. It was then found that, unlike animal cells, bacteria cells have firm walls. So they were called plants. But now scientists call bacteria (and some other tiny organisms) *protists*—not animals or plants, but with features of both.

Bacteriologists—biologists who study bacteria—place these tiny living things into three main groups according to their shapes. Rod-shaped bacteria are called *bacilli*. Ball-shaped bacteria are called *cocci*. And spiral bacteria are called *spirilla*. These living things are so tiny that it would take as many as 50,000 of them to cover one square inch (6.4 sq. cm).

Each bacterium is a single cell. It contains protoplasm and is enclosed by a firm layer, the *cell wall*. Many bacteria can move about by means of

Francis Bacon said that three inventions had changed the world. They were printing, gunpowder, and the compass.

▲ Roger Bacon, English scientist and philosopher.

◀ One of the many subjects Roger Bacon studied was optics. Through his experiments on light and vision, he showed how lenses could be used to help people with weak sight. Spectacles for long-sighted people were first worn about 1285.

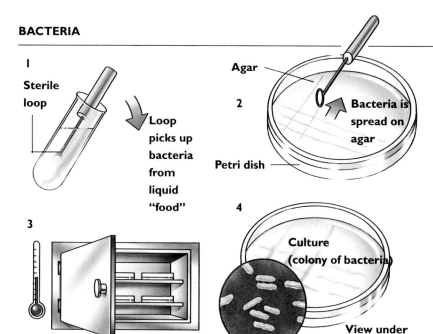

I
Sterile loop

Loop picks up bacteria from liquid "food"

Agar

2
Petri dish

Bacteria is spread on agar

3

Incubator

4
Culture (colony of bacteria)

View under microscope

▲ A process used by scientists to identify bacteria. A sterile loop of wire is used to collect a sample (1), which is smeared in lines on agar (a nutritious jelly) in a petri dish (2). After incubation at a controlled, warm temperature (3) the bacteria colonies grow and show up in the dish (4).

▼ A bacterium is too small to be seen by the naked eye. This is an example of a typical bacterium as seen through a microscope. This bacterium has flagella to help it move.

A TYPICAL BACTERIUM

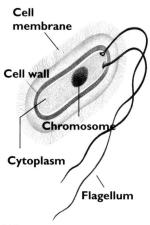

Cell membrane

Cell wall

Chromosome

Cytoplasm

Flagellum

flagella, tiny hairlike threads. Other bacteria do not have flagella and must be carried about by wind, water, or other means.

Bacteria reproduce by simple *fission* (division). One cell splits into two, and two into four, and so on. A mass of bacteria is called a *colony*. One bacterium could produce several billion more bacteria—or as many people as there are in the world—in less than a day if none of the cells died. Fortunately, many cells die.

Some bacteria die if they are dried out. Others die when they are cold. Heat kills bacteria, but some kinds of bacteria form hard covers and become *spores*. These bacteria can live for several hours even in boiling water.

Some bacteria need oxygen. But others, called *anaerobic* bacteria, die if they come into contact with oxygen. Bacteria that live freely in oxygen are *aerobic*. Bacteria feed on organic matter. *Saprophytes* eat dead animals and plants. Dead organisms would pile up and take the room that living things need if it were not for these bacteria. Bacteria that live within living animals and plants and harm them while getting food from them are *parasites*. Other bacteria can make some of their own food from inorganic substances.

Some bacteria cause serious diseases, including cholera, tetanus,

tuberculosis, leprosy, scarlet fever, diphtheria, and some types of pneumonia. Bacteria may act in three ways: (1) by *direct action* to destroy tissues, as in tuberculosis; (2) by *mechanical effects*, as when a clump of bacteria blocks a blood vessel; and (3) by producing chemical poisons or *toxins* as in typhoid fever.

In 1880, Louis Pasteur, a French scientist, discovered that if weakened or dead bacteria are injected into animals, the animals are able to resist diseases caused by these bacteria. This discovery led to the prevention of many diseases by *vaccination*.

Most bacteria are not harmful. In fact, life could not continue without many kinds of bacteria. Bacteria that live in soil cause dead plants and animals to *decompose* (break down) into the chemical elements of which they are made. The process of decomposition frees nitrates and other important substances used by living plants and the animals that eat the plants. The cycle of life goes on when those organisms die.

Other useful bacteria live in the digestive systems of people and animals. Bacteria in the stomachs of grass-eating animals break down *cellulose,* the material that forms the stiff walls of plant cells. The work of such bacteria allows cows to digest grass, one step in the production of milk. Other bacteria can ferment the milk, a necessary process in the making of cheese, butter, buttermilk, and yogurt. Still other bacteria are used to eat away the shells of coffee and cacao beans. And other kinds of bacteria may stop the harmful bacteria that cause cavities in teeth, for example. Some bacteria can be altered in the laboratory so they produce useful substances such as medicines.

▶▶▶▶ **FIND OUT MORE** ◀◀◀◀
Cheese; Childhood Diseases; Contagious Diseases; Disease; Herbivore; Immunity; Pasteur, Louis; Plant Diseases; Protist

BADGER

SEE WEASEL

BADLANDS

A rough, barren wilderness, about the size of Delaware, lies in southwestern South Dakota near the Black Hills. Native Americans gave it a name that meant "the Badlands." If you go there, you can stand atop a hill and gaze at mile after mile of jagged ravines and rugged masses of stone. After sundown, the moonlight casts harsh shadows across the land.

Rain in the Badlands usually comes as heavy downpours. For centuries, the water has washed loose dirt and rock down from the Black Hills. The material has collected in the lowland below the hills. Storms and streams cut weird gullies through the soft clay and sandstone, and these are deepened by continuous erosion. Blue, pink, green, and tan minerals add color to the basically gray rock.

Prairie dogs, rabbits, and coyotes live on the edges of the Badlands. Much larger animals lived there about 24 million years ago. Fossils of saber-toothed tigers, rhinoceroses, and three-toed horses have been found preserved in the clay.

▶▶▶▶ **FIND OUT MORE** ◀◀◀◀
Erosion; South Dakota

BADMINTON

Badminton is a game that is like tennis in some ways. The players use *rackets* to bat an object over a net. The game is played on *a court*, although a badminton court is smaller than a tennis court. The net is strung between two poles, with its top 5 feet (1.5 m) above the ground. Badminton is often an indoor sport but can be played on a lawn if there is no

wind. It can be played by two people (*singles*) or four (*doubles*).

A badminton racket is smaller and lighter than a tennis racket. The handle is slimmer, and the head is much smaller. A lighter racket is used because the badminton player must be able to make shots very quickly with a snap of the wrist.

The game is played by *volleying* (hitting) a *shuttlecock*, called a "bird," over the net without letting it touch the ground. The bird is a small rounded cork or rubber object with a bunch of feathers (real or more usually plastic) attached to its back.

Only the side serving the bird can score a point. When the opponent allows the bird to touch the ground, hits it out of the playing area, into or under the net, or allows himself to be touched by the bird, the serving side is awarded a point. The first side to score 15 points wins the game.

Skillful players can control the bird and place their shots. They can lob the bird behind the opponent, drop it gently just over the net, or smash it straight past the opponent.

Badminton, or *poona*, was brought to England from India about 1870 and was played at the Duke of Beaufort's estate, called *Badminton*. The sport quickly spread throughout England and to other countries.

▶▶▶▶ **FIND OUT MORE** ◀◀◀◀
Sports; Tennis

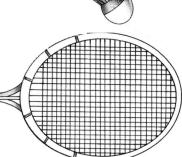

▼ The shuttlecock, or bird, has a cork or rubber head to which up to 16 feathers are attached.

▲ A badminton racket is made of steel or carbon fiber. It is light enough to be swung with a flick of the wrist.

◀ The Badlands of South Dakota form a landscape of many different colors and shapes. Little grows there beside a few wildflowers and sagebrush.

▲ Badminton players usually wear white clothing.

BAGPIPE

Musicians played the strange instrument called the *bagpipe* long before Christ was born. The Roman Emperor Nero played the ancient instrument, and the Roman army probably marched through Europe to its music. The bagpipe was popular all over Europe in the Middle Ages. Today, people in Ireland, France, Spain, and India play the bagpipe, but it is known chiefly as the national instrument of Scotland.

A Scottish bagpipe consists of a bag, usually a sheepskin, and several reed pipes. The player blows into the *blowpipe* and fills the bag with air. As he continues to blow, the air is forced into the melody pipe, or *chanter*. To play a tune, the player puts his fingertips over holes in the chanter. Air is forced into several other pipes, too. These are called *drone* pipes. Most bagpipes have three drone pipes, each of which produce a different, continuous note. The drone notes make a background for the melody.

The bagpipe produces a strange, shrill tone, called a *skirl*. It often led Scottish armies into battle. Bagpipes are also used to play *pibrochs*, traditional songs with many variations, and music for folk dances such as the *Highland fling*.

▶▶▶▶ **FIND OUT MORE** ◀◀◀◀
Music; Musical Instruments; Scotland

▲ **A Scottish piper of the 1600s. Pipers often led their armies into battle. They hoped that the dramatic sound of the bagpipes would frighten off their enemies.**

BAHAMAS

SEE WEST INDIES

BAHRAIN

SEE ARABIA

BAIRD, JOHN LOGIE (1888–1946)

John Logie Baird was a Scottish inventor and one of the pioneers of television. He was born in Helensburgh, Scotland, and he attended the University of Glasgow. In 1922, Baird began to think about *transmitting* (sending) pictures across great distances. Using a mechanical system (rather than the electronic system later adopted as standard), Baird transmitted the first crude television pictures in 1924. These pictures showed only the outlines of objects. But Baird quickly developed his new invention. He was soon able to send clear TV pictures of human faces. He gave a public demonstration of the first true television at the Royal Institution in London, on January 27, 1926.

He also invented a *noctovisor*, for seeing in darkness and through fog, using infrared light. Baird transmitted his first color picture in 1928, and developed clear, brilliant pictures in natural color by 1939. He devoted the last years of his life to trying to discover how to transmit three-dimensional television pictures.

▶▶▶▶ **FIND OUT MORE** ◀◀◀◀
Television; Zworykin, Vladimir

▶ **Baird's 30-line "televisor" of 1930 came four years after he successfully demonstrated television. In the end, however, Baird's system lost out to the rival electronic system invented by Vladimir Zworykin.**

BAKING AND BAKERIES

Bread was the first food to be made, rather than gathered. People all over the world have been bread bakers for thousands of years—long before written history. Until the 20th century, most people baked their own bread at home. The first breads were probably made of nuts or wild grass seeds pounded between two stones. People slowly learned to farm, and they raised large crops of grain—wheat, rye, millet, barley, oats, and corn—for bread. People learned to change the taste and texture of grain by changing the way it is *milled* (ground). Milling separates the *flour*, or food part of grain, from the *bran*, or seed coat. Millers today can make about 150 different flours by changing the grinding process.

Early bread was not like the bread you are probably used to. It was flat, heavy, and dry. It looked and tasted something like Mexican tortillas. Archeologists have found a piece of such bread over 4,000 years old in the ruins of an ancient village in Switzerland.

The bread that people eat most often today is baked from *fermented* dough, which contains bubbles of *carbon dioxide,* a gas. The bubbles expand when the dough is heated, and the bread *rises,* becoming light and airy. Dough ferments if it stands before it is baked. But this takes a long time, so bakers often add *yeast,* a tiny plant that releases carbon

LEARN BY DOING

Why not make your own yeast bread at home? This recipe will make 18 bread rolls. Dissolve 1 package of yeast in one cup of lukewarm water. Put into a bowl ¼ cup soft butter, ¼ teaspoon salt, and 2 tablespoons sugar. Add the yeast-and-water mixture to the mixture in the bowl. Mix all these ingredients; stir in one cup of boiling water. Add one egg and stir it in until blended. Add 2¾ cups of sifted flour. Mix thoroughly to form a soft dough.

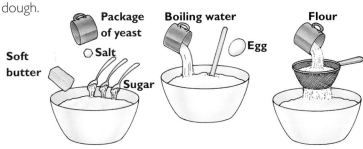

Put the dough in a large bowl that is greased inside. Then turn the dough over so that the upper side is greased. Cover with aluminum foil. Refrigerate at least two hours, or overnight.

When you are ready to bake the rolls, take out the dough and punch it down with your fist. Shape the rolls. Grease muffin pans with shortening or vegetable oil. Fill the pans to one-third full. Cover the pans with a clean cloth and allow the dough to rise in a warm place free from drafts. Let dough rise until doubled in size. Bake in the oven 15 to 18 minutes at 425°F (220°C). Take them out of the pans at once. Spread rolls with butter or jam.

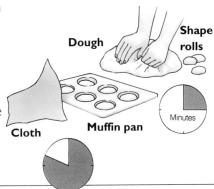

dioxide into the dough. It speeds up the *leavening* (rising) process. The ancient Egyptians probably discovered this by accident when some yeast cells were blown through the air and landed on unbaked dough. The process of *kneading* (folding, pressing, and stretching dough with the hands) is often required for breads made with yeast. Some examples of modern yeast breads are coffee cakes, rolls, and sweet breads.

Bakers sometimes add baking powder, baking soda, or both, to dough instead of yeast. Such dough rises as it bakes, so it does not have to stand

◄ **When the Roman city of Pompeii (destroyed in A.D. 79) was excavated in the 18th century, a bakery complete with oven and loaves of bread was discovered.**

> The longest loaf of bread ever baked was 2,357 feet (718 m) long. It was baked in 1987 in Vergennes, Vermont.

as yeast dough does. Breads made this way are called *quick breads,* and include biscuits, muffins, and fruit breads.

Bread today contains more ingredients than flour, salt, leavening, and water, which were the basic ingredients of ancient bread. Today's bread may contain sweetening, shortening, and sometimes milk. Some commercial bakers *enrich,* or add vitamins and minerals, to bread. Softening

▲ Modern commercial bakeries have machines that produce hundreds of loaves at a time. These bakeries must be kept very clean to meet local health standards.

substances and chemicals called *preservatives* may be added to make and keep bread soft. Baked foods become stale quickly if preservatives are not added.

Other sweet foods were also made by early bakers. Cakes are mentioned in the Bible, and some have even been found in ancient Egyptian tombs. Today, huge quantities of cakes, pies, cookies, and pastries are made and eaten each year.

Commercial Bakeries
Although bread-baking machines for home use have become popular in recent years, bread baking is not often done in homes today. Why? Because it is possible to purchase a wide variety of breads from commercial bakeries. Bakeries use three different processes to make bread—the

sponge process, the *dough* process, and the *continuous-mix* process.

Most large commercial bakeries in the U.S. use the sponge process. Machines do most of the work. To make the sponge, which is the dough, flour is first measured. Then yeast, vitamins, minerals, and water are added to it. The sponge mixture is poured into a huge steel trough. The dough ferments for about 5 hours at 78°F (25.5°C), until it rises. Next the fermented dough is mixed by machine with water, sugar, shortening, butter, eggs, milk, and preservatives. Another machine cuts this mixture and rolls it into balls which are flattened and kneaded. Then the machine shapes the dough into loaves and puts them into pans. The pans are put into a huge, warm *proof box,* where the loaves rise. After rising, the loaves are baked in very long, tunnel-like ovens at 450°F (232°C) for over 25 minutes. The loaves usually travel on a slow conveyor belt as they bake. After they are finished, they are moved to machines for slicing and wrapping.

Usually only small bakeries use the dough process to make bread. The kind of dough that is made is more difficult to move through machinery, so the mixing, shaping, and kneading are usually done by hand. All the ingredients are mixed together only one time. The dough ferments only about three hours. More yeast is used in this process than in the sponge process. All of the flour ferments, so the bread has a stronger flavor, firmer texture, and harder crust than bread made from sponge dough.

In the continuous-mix process, a liquid mixture is made that contains part of the flour plus all the other ingredients used to make bread. This mixture is fermented in huge tanks. After fermenting, the mixture is pumped into a continuous-mix machine. The machine blends this mixture with the rest of the flour to make dough. Next the machine pours the same amount of dough into several thousand pans for baking. The bread made by this process is very soft and smooth.

▶▶▶▶ **FIND OUT MORE** ◀◀◀◀
Fermentation; Flour Making; Food Processing; Grain; Nutrition; Yeast

BALANCE OF NATURE

SEE ECOLOGY

BALBOA, VASCO NUNEZ DE (1475–1519)

Vasco Núñez de Balboa was the first European to see the eastern shore of the Pacific Ocean, in 1513.

Balboa was born in Spain but spent about ten years on a Caribbean plantation before helping to start a colony at Darien (now in Panama). Instead of killing the Natives as did most Spanish *conquistadores* (conquerors), Balboa made some of them his friends. However, he could also be cruel to get what he wanted.

He heard from the Natives about a great sea and a land of gold. He formed an expedition of about 100 Spaniards and 1,000 Natives. For more than three weeks they fought their way through dense jungle and across deep rivers. At last, Balboa crawled wearily to the top of a high hill and looked out. There he saw the sparkling blue Pacific Ocean.

Balboa did not live to know the size of the "Southern Sea," as he called it. He was beheaded a few years later by a Spanish governor of Darien known as Pedrarias. Panama's coin, the *balboa*, is named for him. And when the United States built the Panama Canal, the Pacific entrance city was named Balboa.

▶▶▶▶ **FIND OUT MORE** ◀◀◀◀
Conquistador; Exploration; Pacific Ocean; Panama

BALDWIN, JAMES (1924–1987)

James Baldwin was a black American author best known for his novels and essays about racial conflict in the United States. He was born and raised in the slums of Harlem in New York City. He went to work in factories after graduating from high school, but he used his evenings for writing. He won a grant in 1948 that enabled him to live and work in Europe. His first book, *Go Tell It on the Mountain,* was published in 1953 and was an instant success. It is the story of a 14-year-old black boy growing up in Harlem. It was followed by a group of essays, *Notes of a Native Son* (1955).

Baldwin returned to the U.S. in 1957 and became active in the civil rights movement. He also continued to turn out best-selling books such as *Nobody Knows My Name* (essays) and *Another Country* (a novel). One of his outstanding collections of essays, *The Fire Next Time,* criticizes American society for the way it treats black citizens. In 1965, Baldwin wrote the play *Blues for Mr. Charlie* that was performed on Broadway.

▶▶▶▶ **FIND OUT MORE** ◀◀◀◀
Civil Rights Movement

▶ **Vasco Núñez de Balboa, the Spanish explorer, sighted the Pacific Ocean from a mountain on the Isthmus of Panama in 1513. He claimed the Pacific Ocean for Spain, naming the new ocean the Great Southern Sea.**

▲ **Novelist James Baldwin wrote about what it means to be black in America.**

LEARN BY DOING

Balboa strode into the sea carrying the flag of Spain. He claimed for Spain all the land that this sea touched. Find the Pacific Ocean on a globe or map of the world. Count how many countries that would mean that Spain could own!

In the court game of pelota, or "jai alai," balls are hurled at incredible speeds. The fastest ever recorded speed is 188 miles per hour (302 km/hr).

▼ Balls are used in many different sports and games and come in a variety of shapes and sizes.

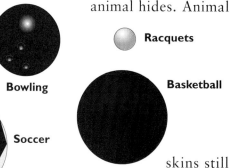

Football

Bowling

Racquets

Basketball

Baseball

Cricket

Soccer

Lacrosse

Golf

Softball

Tennis

Crocquet

Ping-Pong

The first ballet performed in America was in New York in 1827. The audience, shocked at how little clothing the dancers wore, walked out.

BALL

The first toy balls were probably rounded stones, which were rolled or tossed. Thousands of years ago, balls were used as weapons. They were thrown at enemies and game animals.

Balls are rolled, tossed, and hit in many games. Baseball, basketball, tennis, bowling, volleyball, billiards, golf, and many other games use balls of some kind. We usually think of a ball as perfectly *spherical*, or round. This is not always so. A football, for example, is oval instead of round.

Balls can be made of almost any material, including snow. The Aztecs and Mayans played an old game like basketball with a rubber ball. Native North Americans played lacrosse and other games with balls made of animal hides. Animal skins still provide the covering for some kinds of balls. Cowhide is the outer surface of most baseballs. Plastics are now widely used in making different kinds of balls. Others are made of solid wood, rubber, cork, animal hair, and string.

There are many sizes and weights of balls. Maybe you have seen a big, heavy, sand-filled "medicine" ball in a gym. Compare that with a light-weight table tennis ball. One of the smallest balls is the kind used in a game of jacks. It must be tiny enough to fit in a child's hand. It must also be bouncy enough to give the player time to pick up the jacks. Today, balls for each sport have a standard shape, size, and weight.

▶▶▶▶ **FIND OUT MORE** ◀◀◀◀
Sports

BALLAD

SEE FOLK SONG

BALLET

Many people think that ballet dancing is one of the most beautiful arts. Steps and movement are put together with music, costume, and scenery to entertain an audience. Some parts of a ballet are danced by a group, others by one or two main dancers. The ballet often tells a story, but it does not have to.

▲ The French artist, Edgar Degas, is famous for his pictures of dancers at a ballet school. This striking painting, finished in about 1888, is called *Dancers at the Bar*.

Learning the Steps

Both boys and girls study ballet and learn the same steps. It may take as long as ten years to learn to control the body and do the steps. Dancers must also learn a language of gesture, or *pantomime*.

There are five basic positions of the feet that a dancer must learn. All the dance movements begin and

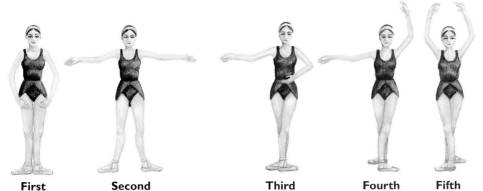

| First | Second | Third | Fourth | Fifth |

▼ Dancers Margot Fonteyn
and Rudolf Nureyev dazzled
audiences all over the
world with their stunning
performances together.

end in one of these positions. There are six main movements: bending, stretching, raising, sliding, darting, and turning. They have French names because the movements were developed in France. Ballet dancers, in whichever country they live, use these French names.

A girl dancer must learn the very difficult art of dancing on her toes, or *sur les pointes*. Ballet shoes have a hard block at the toes, on which the dancers stand. Dancers even darn the toes of the shoes so that the extra roughness guards against slipping.

Boys learn a variety of different jumps and leaps. All begin and end in one of the five basic foot positions. There are many small jumps. But the *grand jeté* is a long leap through the air. The *entrechat* is a jump straight up, with the feet changing position very rapidly in the air. The feet seem to be "twinkling" when they change position as many as eight times before the dancer lands.

Ballet students aren't the only ones who practice. The most famous ballet dancers spend long hours each day practicing their moves and keeping their bodies in good condition.

Story of the Ballet

A lavish entertainment was put on to celebrate a wedding in the royal French court at Versailles, in 1581. For the first time, dance and music were combined to act out a story. This *ballet de cour* (court ballet) was the beginning of the art of ballet. Opera was developing at the same time. Both as dance and as part of

opera, ballet became popular. King Louis XIV of France sometimes performed in ballets. He so loved the art that he started the Royal Academy of Dance in 1661.

Ballet developed over the next 200 years and spread to other European countries. The major steps and movements which are still used were established, and the special hard-toed shoe for toe dancing was invented. Audiences especially liked the romantic love story ballets, such as *Giselle* and *La Sylphide*.

The czars (emperors) of Russia enjoyed ballet. Russian composers wrote music especially for the dance. Peter Tchaikovsky, one of the first major composers of ballet music, wrote *Swan Lake*, *Sleeping Beauty*, and *Nutcracker*. These ballets are still widely performed. Children especially enjoy seeing *Nutcracker*, a Christmas story, during the holiday season.

▼ A scene from the ballet *La Fille Mal Gardée*, or *The Unchaperoned Daughter*. It is a modern version of an old ballet.

Modern Ballet

A young Russian, Sergei Diaghilev of the Ballet Russe, was interested in modern art and music in the early 20th century. He felt that great ballet was more than just great dancing. He turned to such young composers as Igor Stravinsky and Maurice Ravel for new music. Famous artists, such as Pablo Picasso, made costumes and scenery designs for the Ballet Russe. Diaghilev incorporated the informal modern dance into the formal classical ballet, giving new ballets a freshness and a sense of excitement.

In 1909, Diaghilev took the Ballet Russe to Paris. The performances were a sensation. One reason for the Ballet Russe's success was that the great Russian dancer, Anna Pavlova, performed with the group. One of the young male dancers was Vaslav Nijinsky. His amazing skill and grace were such that he is remembered as one of the great dancers of all time.

The Ballet Russe started the age of modern ballet. The Sadler's Wells Ballet, later called the Royal Ballet, was formed in England in the 1930s. One of its great dancers, Dame Margot Fonteyn, later danced with Rudolf Nureyev, a Soviet dancer who sought refuge in the West in 1961. Russia trains many fine dancers who perform with leading companies such as the Bolshoi Ballet. Many other countries have national ballet companies that perform colorful ballets based on their nation's folktales, besides the well-known classical and modern ballets.

There have been several important American ballet companies. One is the New York City Ballet. Its choreographer, George Balanchine, created many beautiful classical and modern ballets. American Ballet Theater is another leading U.S. company. Others include Dance Theater of Harlem and Ballet West. Ballet has found its way into musical comedy, beginning with *On Your Toes* in 1939. Agnes de Mille created truly American ballets, such as *Rodeo* and *Fall River Legend*. Many ballets now combine American jazz and rock music with classical movements, bringing ballet to a wider audience.

▶ ▶ ▶ ▶ **FIND OUT MORE** ◀ ◀ ◀ ◀
Dance; Duncan, Isadora; Modern Dance; Nijinsky, Vaslav; Pavlova, Anna; Tchaikovsky, Peter Ilyich

⚙ BALLOON

Have you ever blown up a toy balloon and watched it float in the air? It probably came down almost at once, because it was heavier than air. But if you could have heated the air in the balloon, it might have risen to the ceiling. Hot air weighs less than normal, or cold air, so the balloon would have floated up.

Two French brothers, Joseph and Jacques Montgolfier, and their sister Marianne, who lived in France during the 18th century, watched smoke and small bits of ash rise up the chimney of a fireplace. They realized that hot air is lighter than cold air. Joseph borrowed some silk cloth from his landlady and made a big bag with a hole in one end. He held the hole over a fire. The bag swelled up and floated to the ceiling. Joseph had invented the *hot-air balloon*.

▲ Modern dance is very different from classical ballet. Modern dancers often strike angular, twisted body shapes, as opposed to the flowing lines of classical ballet.

WHERE TO DISCOVER MORE

Klein, Norma. *Baryshnikov's Nutcracker*. New York: Putnam, 1983.
Krementz, Jill. *A Very Young Dancer*. New York: Knopf, 1976.

▲ Sports ballooning is a popular modern pastime. Enthusiasts enjoy the fun of silent, floating flight.

G-ZUMP

Joseph, Jacques, and Marianne then made a balloon out of linen, more than 100 feet (30 m) around. They lined it with paper, so the air would not leak out. They built a big fire in the marketplace at Annonay, France, on June 5, 1783. They filled the balloon with hot air. The crowd was amazed that eight men had to hold the balloon down. When the men let go, the balloon rose over 950 feet (300 m), and after the air cooled, it came gently down more than one mile (1.6 km) away.

Jacques soon built another large balloon. It had a basket underneath for a fire so the air would stay hot inside the bag. Under the basket was a cage for a duck, a rooster, and a sheep. The King and Queen of France watched as the balloon took off in front of the Royal Palace, on September 19, 1783. The balloon flew for eight minutes and traveled a mile and a half (2.4 km).

The brothers sent up another balloon on November 21, 1783. The balloon carried two people, Jean-Francois Pilatre de Rozier and the Marquis of Arlandes. They flew 5 miles (8 km) in 25 minutes and became the first true aviators.

At about the same time J.A.C. Charles, also French, discovered how to fill balloons with *hydrogen*. Hydrogen is a gas even lighter than hot air, so his balloons could fly longer and higher. Professor Charles's first manned balloon flight was on December 1, 1783.

Hydrogen is dangerous because just a small spark makes an air-hydrogen mixture explode. But it was used in balloons and airships until *helium* was discovered many years later. Helium is also a lighter-than-air gas, but it does not explode.

Ballooning quickly became very popular all over the world. Many contests were held to see whose balloon could go fastest, highest, or farthest. Armies used balloons in wars. They were usually tied to the ground

and flown like kites. The man on board was high in the air, so he could see what the enemy was doing and tell his army. *Observation* balloons like this were used by both the Union and Confederate forces during the Civil War. Moored balloons were used for defense against low-flying bombing planes in World War II.

▲ Barrage balloons were used by the British during World War II. The giant balloons were anchored to the ground with ropes. They were a defense against low-flying enemy planes.

LEARN BY DOING

To make your own hot-air balloon, you need sheets of tissue paper and glue. Cut out the shape shown in the picture below (left) from a piece of tissue paper, or glue one square and four rectangles together. Glue the long sides of the paper shape together to make your "balloon." Put a small candle or flashlight in a jar and light it very carefully. Put the balloon over the jar. As the air heats up, the balloon will rise.

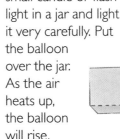
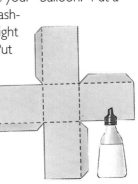

In 1978, three Americans, Ben Abruzzo, Max Anderson, and Larry Newman, became the first balloonists to cross the Atlantic Ocean. Their balloon, the *Double Eagle II,* soared from Presque Isle, Maine, to a field near Paris, France.

▼ **A holiday resort in Germany on the shores of the Baltic Sea.**

The experience gained with balloons helped aviators to build large, steerable *airships*. But balloons were still useful. Huge, unmanned plastic balloons now collect weather information and carry scientific instruments that relay measurements to the ground by radio. They fly as high as 50,000 feet (15,000 m) and can go around the world many times before they wear out. Balloons also measure winds, temperature, pressure, and humidity.

The first space balloon, Echo I, was inflated in space at a height of more than 1,000 miles (1,609 km) above the Earth by NASA in 1960. It was used to locate and track communication satellites.

Sport ballooning has become a hobby, particularly in the United States. Hot-air balloons have burners fed by bottled gas to heat the air. A pilot turns on the burner to heat the air and make the balloon rise higher.

Balloonists have flown the Atlantic and Pacific oceans, and reached a height of 101,520 feet (30,942 m) above the ground.

▶▶▶▶ **FIND OUT MORE** ◀◀◀◀
Air; Airship; Aviation

BALTIC SEA

Ships can sail from the Atlantic Ocean deep into northern Europe by way of the Baltic Sea. The Baltic Sea is 930 miles (1,496 km) long and 400 miles (643 km) across at its widest part. The sea is fairly shallow, averaging about 300 feet (91 m) deep. (See the map with the article on EUROPE.)

A ship must navigate a narrow channel off the Danish coast to get to the Baltic from the North Sea. The ship can then travel as far east as St. Petersburg in Russia, or as far north as Kemi in Finland. It can stop along the way in Denmark, Sweden, Germany, Poland, and the three Baltic republics of Estonia, Latvia,

and Lithuania. The busy ports of Copenhagen (Denmark), Stockholm (Sweden), and Gdansk (Poland) are on Baltic shores.

The Kiel Canal is a shortcut from the Baltic to the North Sea, across the narrow neck of Germany. Other canals join the Baltic with the Arctic Ocean and the Volga River.

▶▶▶▶ **FIND OUT MORE** ◀◀◀◀
Denmark; North Sea

BAMBOO

Bamboo is a type of grass that grows so tall that it looks like a tree. Its fast-growing stems can be used for food, clothing, building, and even to reinforce concrete. Household items made of bamboo include fishing rods, baskets, cooking steamers, and decorative screens. Bamboo is lightweight and inexpensive.

There are about 700 species of bamboo. Two of these are native to southeastern states, such as Georgia and Florida. Most of the world's

▲ **Bamboo has hundreds of uses. Its hollow shoots can be made into all sorts of things, from cups to bird cages and baskets. Bamboo also makes a strong, but light, building material.**

bamboo products come from the tropical countries of Asia, where the tallest bamboos grow. Some of these reach heights of 120 feet (37 m) above the forest floor and their stems can measure up to 39 inches (1m) around.

Bamboo shoots grow quickly, reaching their full height in several months. Some species grow as much as 36 inches (90 cm) in 24 hours. Their hollow stems are smooth, with thick joints to provide support. Mature bamboos have few leaves.

Bamboo's combination of quick growth, light weight, and strength makes it an ideal building material for people in tropical countries. Many houses, including the plumbing, are made completely out of bamboo.

BANDS

SEE ORCHESTRAS AND BANDS

BANGLADESH

This Asian nation came into being in 1971. Before then it was called East Pakistan and was one of the two widely separate regions making up the Muslim country of Pakistan. East Pakistan was the poorer of the two. Its Bengali people demanded greater self-government and aid for their region from the richer West Pakistan. This protest led to rebellion, and West Pakistan sent troops to restore order. But the Indian army helped the Bengalis, who defeated the West Pakistanis and won their independence in 1971. *Bangladesh* (Bengal nation) was born.

Bangladesh has few natural resources, other than its land and water. Poor food production and serious overcrowding have led to periods of famine. Martial law (law administered by military forces) was

imposed from 1982 to 1986. The first proper democratic elections were held in 1991.

Bangladesh, on the Bay of Bengal, is about the size of Wisconsin. The biggest cities are the capital, Dhaka, and the main port, Chittagong. The climate is hot and humid. In the rainy season, branches of the Ganges and Brahmaputra rivers flood the flat land. Cyclones and tidal waves coming from the bay often inflict damage in the delta region. In 1991, the worst cyclone since Bangladesh became independent killed more than 130,000 people.

Almost all of the people live in small farming villages. Many animals such as tigers, elephants, and water buffaloes, live in the forests. Rice, jute (used to make twine and sacks), tea, and sugarcane are the main crops. Freshwater and saltwater fishing are also important.

▶▶▶▶ **FIND OUT MORE** ◀◀◀◀
Ganges River; India; Pakistan

BANGLADESH

Capital city
Dhaka (4,770,000 people)

Area
55,598 square miles
(143,999 sq. km)

Population
113,005,000 people

Government
Multi-party republic

Natural resources
Farmland, fish

Export products
Jute, leather, tea, fish, hides and skins

Unit of money
Taka

Official language Bengali
(English is also spoken)

▲ The Bank of England, founded in 1694, served as a model for many later banks.

There was not a single bank in America before the Revolution. People just borrowed money from each other.

▶ The first coins, made of electrum, were used in Turkey in about 700 B.C.

▼ Banks invest the money deposited with them in bonds and stock shares. These are sold in a stock exchange, the first of which (shown here) opened in Amsterdam in 1612.

BANKS AND BANKING

Before there were any banks, people had to carry money with them if they went on a journey. Imagine that you lived in England centuries ago. You have to travel from London to Plymouth. You do not want to carry many gold coins because there are robbers along the way. So you give your gold coins to a London goldsmith to hold. Goldsmiths always kept their gold and jewels in safe places.

The goldsmith gives you a *receipt*, showing that the goldsmith accepted responsibility for the coins. The goldsmith will return the coins when you come back to London and return the receipt. For this service, you pay a small sum to the goldsmith.

When you reach Plymouth, you need money to buy new clothes. You borrow ten gold coins from a friendly merchant who is going to London. In exchange, you give the merchant a note telling the goldsmith in London to give ten of your gold coins to the merchant. The goldsmith has served as a banker.

Hundreds of years before the birth of Christ, people in Greece and Egypt loaned money to other people. Later, the Romans made laws to control moneylending. But there were no banks like those we have today.

The first real bank was probably the Bank of San Giorgio in Genoa, Italy. It began in 1148. Other banks soon opened in other countries. The first bank in the United States was the Bank of North America, in Philadelphia, in 1782. It was a great success. Two other private American banks opened in 1784, one in New York and one in Boston. In 1791, Congress issued a charter, or permit, for the First Bank of the United States. This bank was in Philadelphia and lasted until 1811, when Congress refused to renew the bank's permit. Hundreds of new banks were then given permits by state governments. The Federal Government set up the *National Banking System* and also issued the first Federal paper money in 1862.

Borrowing, Saving, and Paying

Today, we take banks for granted. They are stores that deal in money. You can borrow money from banks to buy homes, automobiles, or other goods. Towns and cities borrow from banks to build schools and roads. Banks lend money to makers of air-

planes, cars, clothing, and other things. In this way manufacturers can buy supplies, new machines, or put up new buildings. Without banks, factories would close, and millions of people could not pay for goods.

If you borrow money from a bank,

you must pay it back with *interest*. That is, you pay the bank a little more than you borrow. When you *deposit,* or put money in a *savings account* in a bank, the bank pays you interest. It then uses your money to make loans to others. The interest the bank charges for lending money is higher than the interest it pays to depositors, so the bank makes a profit by making loans. Money in a savings account cannot always be taken out, or *withdrawn,* any time the depositor wishes. For some types of accounts, the bank wants advance warning about any withdrawals.

Some banks pay no interest on *checking accounts* because the money in these accounts may not stay in the bank, as savings do. The depositor may write *checks.* A check is a written order telling the bank to pay a certain amount of money to a certain person or company. People with checking accounts do not have to carry large amounts of cash.

Besides lending money, banks also give advice to customers about using their money in helpful ways. For example, people may pay a bank to take care of their money when they die. They arrange to put their money and other property "in trust." They tell the bank how the money is to be

used. When they die, the bank's *trust department* will see that the money is used as they wished.

There are many kinds of banks. *Commercial* banks, which include state and national banks, make loans and investments. *Savings* banks accept time deposits (mutual savings are owned by the depositors). *Central* banks hold the cash reserves of a country. The central banking system of the United States is the Federal Reserve System. It consists of 12 Federal Reserve Banks that make loans to regular state and national banks. They regulate the money of the U.S. government.

All banks must obey special state

or federal banking laws. A number of banking scandals in the late 1980s and early 1990s made people question the effectiveness of banking regulations. Attempts were made to rewrite the laws.

▶ ▶ ▶ ▶ **FIND OUT MORE** ◀ ◀ ◀ ◀
Economics; Money; Savings

If one dollar had been banked 200 years ago and left to accumulate at 10 percent per annum interest, it would now be worth $150 million.

◀ **An English bank note for £555 dated 1699. Although Europe had known of paper money from China since the 13th century, it did not come into use until the 1600s.**

▲ **The inside of a modern-day bank. To withdraw or deposit money in a checking account, a customer fills out a slip and hands it to one of the bank's tellers (behind). Customers can also use automated teller machines to make transactions.**

BANNEKER, BENJAMIN (1731–1806)

Benjamin Banneker was one of the most famous black people in early U.S. history. He was a mathematician, astronomer, and farmer, and published pamphlets against slavery and war.

Banneker was born a freeman in Maryland at a time when most blacks were slaves. His grandmother taught him to read the Bible by the time he was four. He attended a Quaker school and became interested in astronomy. He built a wooden clock that kept nearly perfect time, and he charted the movement of the stars so accurately that he published his own almanac from 1792 until he died.

President George Washington appointed him assistant planner and surveyor for the new capital city. The chief architect was Pierre-Charles L'Enfant, a Frenchman. As a surveyor, Banneker was allowed to see L'Enfant's drawings, which the architect usually kept secret. L'Enfant resigned and Andrew Ellicott replaced him as chief architect. The angry L'Enfant took all of his drawings with him, but Banneker was able to reconstruct the plan from memory.

▶▶▶▶ **FIND OUT MORE** ◀◀◀◀
District of Columbia

▶ **How human insulin is made.** Genes controlling the production of insulin are extracted and then spliced into the genes of a virus. The virus then injects this gene along with its own into a bacterium. The insulin-producing gene now becomes part of the bacterium's genes and it now can reproduce insulin. The bacterium grows by multiplying itself. When enough bacteria have grown they are harvested. The insulin is then separated and purified for use.

▲ Frederick Banting, Canadian medical scientist.

BANTING, FREDERICK (1891–1941)

The disease called *diabetes* used to cause many deaths. But today, people suffering from diabetes can be treated with the hormone *insulin*. The discoverer of insulin was Frederick Banting, a Canadian surgeon.

Besides being a surgeon, Banting worked as an instructor in medicine at the University of Toronto. One evening, while preparing a lecture on a body organ called the *pancreas*, he read an article on the problem of diabetes. Doctors knew that certain glands in the pancreas produce a hormone that helps the body make use of sugar, and that a person would get diabetes if these glands failed to make enough of the hormone. But no one had been able to extract the hormone for use as a medicine.

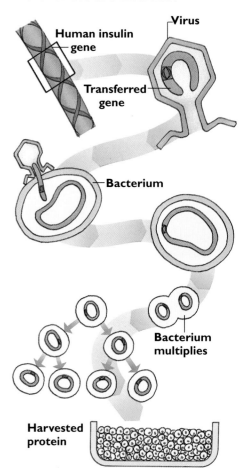

Banting began work on the problem under the direction of the Scottish physiologist, Professor John Macleod. Late in 1921, he succeeded with the help of two assistants, Charles Best and James Collip. The hormone, later called insulin, was tested first on a dog and then on a child dying of diabetes. It worked. Banting and Macleod won the 1923 Nobel Prize in physiology and medicine for their work. Banting shared his award with Best, and Macleod shared his with Collip.

▶▶▶▶ **FIND OUT MORE** ◀◀◀◀
Hormone; Human Body; Medicine

BAPTIST

A Baptist is a member of a Protestant religious group that believes in adult baptism. This practice is reserved for those old enough to accept Jesus Christ as their savior. Baptists form the largest Protestant group in the United States.

The Baptist movement began in England in the early 1600s. Certain clergymen began to criticize the Church of England's practice of baptizing infants and called for less control of beliefs by bishops and other religious authorities. One of these preachers, John Smyth, joined the Pilgrims who fled to Holland before departing for New England.

Baptist beliefs played a large part in the early history of the American colonies. Roger Williams, a Baptist clergyman, founded the colony of Rhode Island in 1636 to secure freedom of worship for the Baptists of New England.

The strong but simple message of the Baptists gained many converts in colonial America. By the time of the Revolution the Baptists had become the largest denomination. They remain the largest Protestant group in the United States, second only to the Roman Catholics overall.

Baptist denominations are called *associations* or *conventions*. The Southern Baptist Convention is the largest in the United States, with nearly 15 million members. There are two major groups for black American Baptists—the National Baptist Convention of America and the National Baptist Convention, U.S.A., Inc. There are more than 27 million Baptists in the United States.

▶ ▶ ▶ ▶ **FIND OUT MORE** ◀ ◀ ◀ ◀
Jackson, Jesse; King Jr., Martin Luther

BARBADOS

SEE WEST INDIES

BAR CODE

When you buy something at a store, have you ever noticed a pattern of black and white stripes on the carton or package? This is called a *bar code*, and it helps the people who run and own the store.

The stripes make a number in a code known as *binary code*. In this code, a thick stripe stands for 1 and a thin stripe for 0. Each product that you buy has a different number. At the store's check-out, a machine "reads" the bar code and converts it into a signal that goes to the store's computer. The computer looks up the price of each item and prepares the sales slip. In addition, it keeps track of how many products are sold every day. It can then work out what new supplies need to be ordered.

When you go shopping, look to see how many different items are marked with bar codes.

▶ ▶ ▶ ▶ **FIND OUT MORE** ◀ ◀ ◀ ◀
Binary System; Computer

▲ Mount Vernon Baptist Church, Indianapolis, Indiana. Baptists are baptized into the church when they are old enough to understand what faith is.

In the state of Arizona, bees have been fitted with tiny bar codes by the Department of Agriculture. The bar codes are glued onto the bees' backs. A bar code reader at the entrance to each hive records the bees' comings and goings and allows scientists to select the most productive bees.

Light pen

Bar code

Light-sensitive semiconductor

7 9314118 6215 3

◀ A bar code contains a digital message, turned into bars. This can be decoded by a light pen or panel.

⚙ BARDEEN, JOHN (1908–1991)

John Bardeen was an American scientist, best known for his work in finding out how different kinds of solids carry electric currents. This is very important, because his work made possible the invention of the *transistor*. The transistor is one of the most important inventions of the 20th century. For one thing. it made possible the modern computer.

With William Shockley and Walter Brattain, Bardeen was awarded the 1956 Nobel Prize in physics for his work on the transistor.

Transistors are tiny electronic devices that can *amplify,* or make stronger electric currents; change alternating current into direct current; and perform such tasks as electronic switching and automatic control. Radios, TVs, and computers contain thousands of transistors on a tiny piece of silicon, called a "chip."

In 1972, John Bardeen won a second Nobel Prize, with Leon Cooper and John Schrieffer, for his work on *superconductivity*—the disappearance of electrical resistance in some metals when they are cooled to very low temperatures.

▶▶▶▶ FIND OUT MORE ◀◀◀◀
Cryogenics; Semiconductor; Transistor

▶ **Before the invention of the transistor, vacuum tubes (1) were used in electronic equipment. In the 1960s, tubes were replaced by the transistor (2), which was smaller, used less energy, and cost less. Since then transistors have become much smaller. Today thousands of transistors can be put on a silicon chip (3).**

▼ **Tree bark is made up of inner bark and outer bark. The outer bark is mostly dead cork cells, which form a protective covering. The inner bark is living tissue. Here more cork cells are produced in the cork cambium, and food is transported in the phloem and stored in the cortex.**

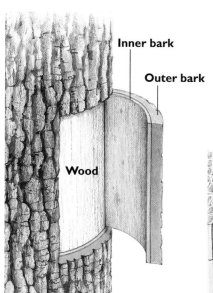

Inner bark

Outer bark

Wood

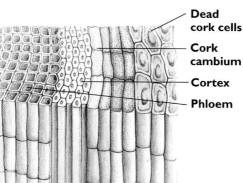

Dead cork cells

Cork cambium

Cortex

Phloem

2
Transistor

Vacuum tube

1

Silicon chip

3

▨ BARK

The outer covering of a tree's trunk and branches is called *bark*. If you know about bark, you can tell what *species,* or type, a tree is, even in winter when the leaves are all gone. Many animals, such as deer and beaver, eat the bark of some trees, and some beetles can tunnel through it.

Some trees have light-colored bark. Trembling aspens and some birches are covered with smooth, white or light-gray bark. The bark on other trees is black or dark brown. A young tree often has bark of a different color from the bark on an old tree of the same type. Some trees have very thin bark. On others, such as the huge Douglas fir, the bark may be more than 12 inches (30 cm) thick.

When you look at a young tree stem, the part you see is a thin protective layer called the *epidermis*. This is soon replaced by *cork,* special tissue made of dead cells whose walls contain waterproof substances. The cork protects the stem from injury, disease, and water loss. The cork splits as the diameter of the stem increases, causing the grooved or peeling appearance of many kinds of bark. This layer of dead cells is often called the *outer bark*.

Just inside the outer cork are the three layers of the *inner bark*. The first of these is the *cork cambium,* which is made up of living cells that add new cork as the stem grows. The second layer is the *cortex*. The cortex of young stems contains *chlorophyll* and manufactures food. But this activity stops when the cork forms, and the cortex is then used to store the food produced by the leaves. The innermost layer of bark is the *phloem,* composed of thin-walled tubes that carry food dissolved in water. The tubes are strengthened by tough fibers called *bast*.

Never pull the bark off a tree, because the growing layer will be damaged. Some trees, however, are grown just for the substances obtained by cutting, or lapping, their bark. *Resins*, sticky substances from pines, are used in turpentine and other products. Rubber is the white, juicy *latex* of the rubber tree.

▶ ▶ ▶ ▶ **FIND OUT MORE** ◀ ◀ ◀ ◀
Plant; Tree

BARLEY

SEE GRAIN

BARNUM, P. T. (1810–1891)

Phineas Taylor Barnum was often called "the world's greatest showman." He was also a pioneer of modern advertising because he used publicity of every kind to draw people to his circus.

Barnum was born in Bethel, Connecticut. He did not have much schooling, but he was smart and

clever at fooling people. He also discovered that many people liked to be fooled.

In his first show he exhibited a midget, known as *General Tom Thumb*. Other famous attractions promoted by Barnum included Jenny Lind, a singer called the "Swedish Nightingale," and Jumbo, a huge African elephant. Barnum put together his first circus in 1871. His main rival, James A. Bailey, later became his partner. Together, they started the Barnum and Bailey Circus, also called "the Greatest Show on Earth." Ringling Brothers bought out the show in the early 1900s.

To advertise his shows, Barnum sent *advance men* ahead of the circus to cover a town with brightly colored posters. Then brass bands and a parade left no one in doubt that the circus had come to town. Above all, he used spectacular words and phrases to describe the wonders of his circus. Barnum was a show-off even in his private life. Whenever a train passed by his home, he would have an elephant out plowing in a nearby field as if to show passengers where the world's greatest showman lived.

▶ ▶ ▶ ▶ **FIND OUT MORE** ◀ ◀ ◀ ◀
Circus

Some trees, including the Mediterranean cork oak, produce very thick bark. This is stripped from the tree at intervals and is the source of commercial cork.

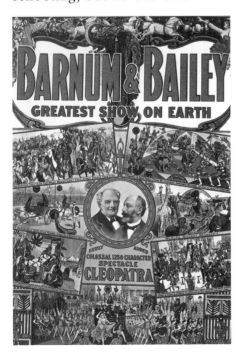

◀ **An early poster for the Barnum and Bailey Circus. Barnum developed a sensational method of advertising called "ballyhoo" to promote his famous traveling circus.**

▲ **Phineas T. Barnum, the great American showman, was so dedicated to show business his dying words were to ask about the day's receipts at the circus.**

◄ **An early barometer, made in the 17th century.**

 # BAROMETER

Barometers are used to measure air pressure and are useful in forecasting the weather. The first barometer was built in 1643 by Evangelista Torricelli, an Italian scientist. He filled a long glass tube, closed at one end, with mercury, and turned it upside down in a bowl of mercury. Air, pressing down on the mercury in the bowl, held the mercury up in the tube. As the air pressure increased, the level of the mercury in the tube rose.

A newer type is the *aneroid* (without air) barometer. It looks like a

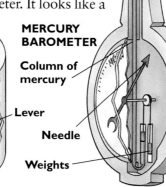

ANEROID BAROMETER

Dial
Needle
Spindle

Vacuum chamber

MERCURY BAROMETER

Column of mercury

Lever

Needle

Weights

▲ **In an aneroid barometer, the vacuum chamber expands or contracts as the air pressure changes, causing the needle to move. In mercury barometers, changes in air pressure cause the liquid mercury to rise or fall by small amounts, which can be read off a scale. Mercury barometers are more accurate than aneroid ones.**

wall clock with a dial and a hand that moves to indicate the air pressure. Behind the dial is a small metal chamber with thin walls. Most of the air has been removed from the chamber. Its sides bend in from the air pressure. The greater the pressure, the more the chamber bends. The bending moves the hand on the dial to give a reading of the pressure.

▶▶▶▶ **FIND OUT MORE** ◄◄◄◄
Air; Air Pressure; Weather

LEARN BY DOING

You can make a barometer to show changes in air pressure. Use a long piece of clear plastic tubing. Suck water part of the way up the tube from a dish. Plug the top with a piece of modeling clay. Stand the tube upright in the dish. Place a scale where the water level is. As the air pressure rises and falls, so will the water level rise and fall. What happens just before a storm?

BAROQUE PERIOD (1600–1750)

"Bursting with life." That might describe Baroque—a period in the arts when much artistic activity was springing into life. In music, we think of the Baroque style as lively, with different melodic lines going on at the same time, and musicians adding ornamental notes and trills. The music of George Frideric Handel (1685–1759) is from the Baroque period. New musical instruments were being designed at this time and the art of the opera was being developed also.

In art, what is called *high Baroque* took place in Italy between 1630 and 1680. The great religious zeal of the time called *the Counter Reformation* was being expressed in big, color-filled paintings showing strong feelings. In addition, many of Europe's rulers tried to glorify their reigns by building magnificent palaces, decorated in the baroque style.

Baroque artists often combined three arts—architecture, painting, and sculpture. The master of all three arts was Giovanni Bernini (1598–1680). He worked for years to help finish the Basilica of Saint Peter in Rome. He combined architecture, painting, and sculpture into one unified form of art.

Baroque paintings were often done on a large scale and were filled with a sense of movement and energy. Paintings were no longer restrained and orderly as they had been in the Renaissance. Instead there was a feeling of infinite space. Many artists were concerned with portraying the inner workings of the mind and attempted to show emotions and personalities.

The great artist Peter Paul Rubens (1577–1640) studied in Italy for eight years just as Baroque was beginning. He then went back to his home in Antwerp (now in Belgium) and made the city a center of European art. His

Triumph of Love (right) is full of energy and golden light. The picture seems to be beyond the limits of the frame, in true Baroque open style.

The architecture of the Baroque period was also full of life. Elements of classical architecture appear, but in a distorted and fantastically decorated form, often creating rich surfaces that catch the sunlight and create interesting shadows. Such exuberance is very Baroque.

The Baroque style in Italy was on a grand scale. It appealed to royalty throughout Europe, and they copied it in their palaces. In France, Baroque is called the style of Louis XIV. He was king of France from 1643 to 1715. In 1661, he began a great monument to himself, the Palace of Versailles. Its Hall of Mirrors, its Trianon and other elaborate features,

fancy, ornate, and covered with *gilt* (gold paint) decoration, speak of a golden period of splendor and spirit.

Look around your city for an example of the Baroque style. Architects have tried to imitate Baroque in auditoriums, theaters, state capitols, and hotel lobbies. They try to give visitors a feeling of elegance. Look for gold decorations, high, domed ceilings, fancy mirrors, statues of cherubs, and large, showy wall pieces. That is Louis XIV style or Baroque. The U.S. Capitol dome is an example of Baroque influence in the United States.

▶ ▶ ▶ ▶ **FIND OUT MORE** ◀ ◀ ◀ ◀
Architecture; Art History; Bach Family; Cathedral; Protestant Reformation; Versailles

▲ **The Triumph of Love by Peter Paul Rubens is a Baroque masterpiece.**

▼ **Bernini's *baldachin* (built between 1624 and 1633) towers above the high altar of Saint Peter's Basilica in Rome. It is typically Baroque in its energy and decoration.**

◀ **David Slaying Goliath by Giovanni Bernini, the leading Italian sculptor and architect of his day. He has been called the creator of the Baroque style in art.**

▲ **Sir James Barrie, Scottish novelist and playwright.**

BARRIE, JAMES M. (1860–1937)

Sir James Matthew Barrie wrote many plays and books. Barrie was born in Kirriemuir, Scotland. His father was a weaver. From the time he was a little boy he wanted to write. Barrie had no children of his own. But he loved the child's world of make-believe and never forgot what fun it is to be very young.

His most famous play is *Peter Pan,* first produced in 1904. *Peter Pan* is the story of a little boy who doesn't want to grow up. He lives in Never-Never Land with Indians, lost boys, pirates, and the fairy Tinker Bell. A little girl named Wendy Darling and her two brothers share Peter's adventures with Captain Hook, a nasty-tempered pirate with a hook for a hand. Barrie gave all the profits from *Peter Pan* to a London children's hospital.

The Little Minister, a novel that Barrie later made into a play, was his first success. Two of Barrie's other well-known plays are *The Admirable Crichton* and *Dear Brutus.*

▶▶▶▶ **FIND OUT MORE** ◀◀◀◀
Children's Literature

BARTON, CLARA (1821–1912)

Clara Barton, the founder of the American Red Cross, was born on a farm in Oxford, Massachusetts. After 18 years of teaching, she was the first woman hired to work as a clerk in the United States Patent Office in Washington, D.C. Miss Barton worked there during the Civil War. She traveled to battlefields in Virginia and Maryland to help the wounded soldiers, who were not getting proper care. Distressed at the conditions she saw, she sought donations of food and delivered meals to the wounded men herself, along with medical supplies. Although she was not a nurse,

▲ **Clara Barton, the soldiers' friend.**

Clara Barton helped treat the soldiers' wounds. Soldiers called her the "Angel of the Battlefields."

Many badly wounded soldiers could not get in touch with their families when the Civil War ended. Clara formed an organization to trace missing people. She soon had files on more than 20,000 people. She worked so hard she became ill, so she went to Europe to rest.

War broke out between France and Prussia (now Germany) in 1870 while Miss Barton was in Europe. Again she nursed the wounded. She also learned about the International Red Cross, a newly founded organization that helped wounded soldiers, prisoners of war, and their families. She returned to the United States in 1881, founded the American Red Cross, and served as its first president. Today, the Red Cross is known for the help it provides in disasters such as earthquakes, hurricanes, or floods.

▶▶▶▶ **FIND OUT MORE** ◀◀◀◀
Red Cross

BASEBALL

One of the most popular sports in the United States is baseball. The game began in the eastern United States in the mid-1880s. It quickly spread throughout the country and became the "national pastime." Today, baseball is very popular in Puerto Rico, Cuba, Japan, Taiwan, Canada, some Latin American countries, and parts of Europe.

In the spring, summer, and fall Americans of all ages play on organized baseball teams. There are high school and college teams; there is *Little League, American Legion, Babe Ruth,* and amateur adult league baseball also.

A *league* is a group of baseball teams that play each other many times during the season. The two major leagues in the U.S. are the American

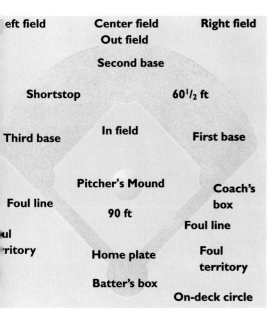

eft field   Center field   Right field
Out field
Second base
Shortstop   60½ ft
Third base   In field   First base
Pitcher's Mound   Coach's
Foul line   box
90 ft   Foul line
ul   Foul
rritory   Home plate   territory
Batter's box
On-deck circle

League and the National League. The teams in these two leagues are made up of some of the world's best baseball players, called *professionals.* The *World Series* is the high point of the professional baseball season. It is really not a world series, but a series of games between the best team from each major league. The winner must win four out of seven games to become the champion team.

History of Baseball
People played games with balls and sticks hundreds of years ago. But their games were not well organized.

People in one town played the game one way, while players in other places used different rules. In 1845, Alexander Cartwright drew the first baseball *diamond.* The first game between two organized teams took place the next year in New Jersey. Some people claim that Abner Doubleday drew up the rules for modern baseball, and that the game was first played in Cooperstown, New York. There is no real proof for this claim. But the Baseball Hall of Fame is now located in Cooperstown.

How to Play
A professional baseball field is called a *diamond,* but it is not diamond-shaped. It is really a square 90 feet (27.4 m) long on each side. At each corner of the square is a *base.* The bases are called *first, second, third,* and *home.* The first three bases are marked by bags. The bags are square in shape and are stuffed canvas. Instead of a bag at home base, there is a flat plate, called *home plate.* The area inside the bases is the *infield.* The area beyond the bases is the *outfield.*

There are nine baseball players on a team. The *first baseman, second baseman,* and *third baseman* guard the bases. The *catcher* stays behind home plate. He guards the plate and catches the ball when the pitcher throws it. The *pitcher* stands on the pitcher's *mound,* a small hill between home plate and second base. The *shortstop* plays the infield between second and third base. The other three players are the *outfielders.* They are the *right fielder,* the *left fielder,* and the *centerfielder.*

Umpires are the officials on the field. They usually wear blue suits and caps. Their job is to decide whether a pitch is a ball or a strike, and whether a player is out or safe. The *manager* of a baseball team is something like a coach. He directs the team and decides which players will be in a game.

◄ The dimensions of a baseball field. The measurements of the infield are always the same although the size of the outfield and foul territory may vary.

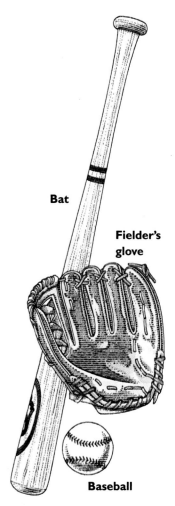

Bat

Fielder's glove

Baseball

▲ The baseball is small and hard, weighing 5 to 5½ ounces (142 and 149 g). The bat is usually made of hardwood and the gloves of leather. There are three kinds of gloves: the catcher's mitt, first baseman's glove, and the fielder's glove.

◄ A baseball player up at bat in the World Series. To become world champions, a team must win four out of seven games in the Series.

331

COMMON TERMS IN BASEBALL

Ball

A pitch that is outside the strike zone

Batting average

The number of hits a player makes divided by the times he has batted

Double header

Two games for the price of one. The games follow one another. Sometimes called a "bargain bill"

Double play

Putting out two players at the same time on one hit

Error

A mistake by a player that allows a runner to be safe when he should have been put out

Fielder's choice

A fielder's decision to put out a runner instead of a batter

Foul ball

A hit by the batter that knocks the ball behind the catcher or off to one side of the field. It counts as a strike against the batter unless he already has two strikes against him

Fly ball

A ball hit high into the air. The batter is out if a player on the opposing team catches the fly ball before it hits the ground

Hit

A batted ball that lets the batter get safely to base

Home run

A ball hit so far that the batter can run around all three bases and return to home plate

Pinch hitter

A substitute for a player who was supposed to bat

Run

Movement around all three bases and to home plate without being put out

Shutout

A game in which one team does not score

Stolen base

Movement of a player to the next base as soon as the ball is pitched, without waiting for the batter to make a hit and without being put out by a baseman

Strike

Failure to hit a good pitch; one that crosses home plate no lower than the batter's knees and no higher than his armpits. This area is called the "strike zone." Also, a foul ball is a strike

Strikeout

Three strikes, which puts the batter out. Also called a "fan" because the batter "fans" the air with his bat

Switch hitter

A batter who can bat from the left or right side of the plate

Walk

Movement to first base after the pitcher has thrown four balls. It is also called "a base on balls"

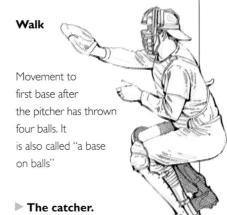

► The catcher.

When a team is in position on the field, the opposing team is *at bat*. The batter stands in front of the opposing catcher and tries to hit the ball when the pitcher throws it. If he swings his bat at the ball and misses, or if he does not swing at a good pitch, he makes a *strike*. But if the pitch is high, low, or off to either side of the plate, and the batter does not swing at it, the pitch is then called a *ball*. When a batter makes three strikes, he is *out*. If a pitcher throws four bad pitches, or balls, the batter *walks*, or moves to first base. When the batting team makes three outs, the other team gets its turn at bat.

The batter sometimes knocks the baseball behind the catcher or off to one side of the field. These balls are called *foul balls*. A foul ball counts as a strike, unless the batter already has two strikes. Balls hit *in bounds* are *fair balls*. A *bunt* is a ball hit lightly into the infield. And a ball hit up in the air is a *fly ball*. The batter is out if a member of the other team catches his fly ball before it hits the ground.

Winning a Game

A baseball game has nine innings. Both teams have a turn at bat in each inning. A *run* is scored when a player touches all four bases. The team with the most runs at the end of nine innings is the winner. If the score is tied, the teams play extra innings, until one team has a higher score than the other team at the end of a full inning.

The object in baseball is for the batter to hit the ball and then reach base. He must reach base before the ball can be picked up, thrown, and caught by the opposing first baseman. A batter may hit the ball so hard that he can run to second or third base before the ball can be thrown to the baseman. He may also hit the ball so far that he can run around all the bases and return to home plate. That is a *home run*.

When a batter gets to first base, he must move to second, third, and then home. He can do this when the next batter makes a hit. The hit may put the new batter on second. When that happens, the runner (the one that was on first) usually can run around the bases and reach home. That scores a run for his team. The other way a runner can move from one base to another is by *stealing* a base. As soon as the ball is pitched, the runner dashes to the next base before a fielder can tag him with the ball to put him out.

A player must do several things well to play good baseball. He must be able to catch the ball when it is thrown or hit to him. He must be able to throw accurately. He must be a good hitter, and he must be a fast runner. The pitcher and catcher work hardest because they are in on every play. The infielders see a lot of action, too. If they are good players, they can make *double plays*. This happens when they throw two opposing players out at the same time. There are also *triple plays*, but they do not happen often. Each person on the team is important to its success, because baseball is a team sport, not an individual sport.

Softball

Softball is similar to baseball, but played with a larger ball on a smaller diamond. Despite the name, the ball used is not soft. Softball rules are a little different from those of baseball.

▲ Baseball attracts big crowds of spectators, and many more fans enjoy watching the games on TV.

SOME MODERN BASEBALL RECORDS

Record	Player	Total	Date
Most home runs in a season	Roger Maris	61	1961
Most home runs in a lifetime	Henry Aaron	755	1954–1976
Highest batting average in a season	Rogers Hornsby	.424	1924
Highest batting average in a lifetime	Ty Cobb	.367	1905–1928
Most strikeouts in a season (pitching)	Nolan Ryan	383	1973
Most strikeouts in a lifetime (pitching)	Nolan Ryan	5,668	1966–1993
Most stolen bases in a season	Rickey Henderson	130	1982
Most stolen bases in a lifetime	Rickey Henderson	939	1979–1991
Most runs in a season	Babe Ruth	177	1921
Most runs in a lifetime	Ty Cobb	2,245	1905–1928
Most games won by a pitcher in a season	Jack Chesbro	41	1904
Most games won by a pitcher in a lifetime	Cy Young	511	1890–1911
Most hits in a season	George Sisler	257	1920
Most hits in a lifetime	Pete Rose	4,256	1963–1986

Basketball got its name because James Naismith, in inventing the game, first planned to have square boxes at each end to receive the ball. He couldn't find suitable boxes and made do with two half-bushel peach baskets instead.

▼ The dimensions of a professional basketball court.

For example, the ball must be pitched underhand and there are seven innings in a regular game. The game of softball began as an indoor sport in Chicago in 1888. Today, it is played mostly outdoors.

▶ ▶ ▶ **FIND OUT MORE** ◀ ◀ ◀
Ball; Gehrig, Lou; Little League Baseball; Robinson, Jackie; Ruth, Babe; Sports

BASES

SEE ACIDS AND BASES

BASILICA

SEE CATHEDRAL

BASKETBALL

Basketball is a very popular spectator sport. Dr. James Naismith, a physical education teacher at what is now Springfield College, Massachusetts, invented the game in 1891. It has become one of the most popular sports in the United States and has spread to other countries. The sport is part of the Olympic Games.

Basketball is an important school sport. Both boys and girls play it. Girls' basketball used to be played differently from boys', but now it follows the same general rules. Most colleges have basketball teams. Top college players often join professional teams after graduation. Many major American cities have professional basketball teams. Millions of people watch these "pro" teams every year.

The Harlem Globetrotters, from New York City, do not play together as a pro team. Instead, they entertain audiences all over the world with fancy ball-handling and skillful playing.

Playing on the Court
Basketball is mainly an indoor activity. The basketball season is during the winter, after football and before baseball. Most high school gyms have at least one basketball court. The court is 84 feet (25.6 m) long and 50 feet (15.2 m) wide. The college and professional court is the same width, but it is 94 feet (28.6 m) long. Basketball players under age 15 use another size court—74 feet (22.5 m) by 42 feet (12.8 m).

At each end of the court is a high, metal hoop with an open-bottomed net hanging from it. This is the *basket* that gives the sport its name. The basket is 18 inches (45.7 cm) wide and 10 feet (3 m) above the floor. The basket is fastened to the *backboard* behind it. The object of the game is to toss, or *shoot*, the ball into the opposing team's basket, or goal. Each team has five players—the *center* (usually the tallest player), two *forwards,* and two *guards*.

Play starts in the middle of the court, with the two opposing centers facing one another. Each team's forwards guard the other team's guards, and the guards guard the opponent's forwards. An official, called the *referee*, throws the ball up between the two centers. This is called a *jump ball*. Both centers leap up and try to tap the ball to a teammate. When you get the ball, your objective is to move the ball in the direction of the

Court diagram labels: 94 ft, 15 ft, Division line, Free-throw circle, 19 ft, Center circle, 12 ft, 50 ft, End line, Backboard, Free-throw line, Restraining circle, Basket, Sideline

other team's basket. You can do this by *passing*, or throwing, the ball to a teammate. You can also do it by *dribbling*, bouncing the ball while you walk or run down the court. Holding the ball in your hands while moving down the court is not allowed. You must pass it to a teammate or shoot at the basket when you stop dribbling.

A basketball player must not commit a *foul* while trying to get the ball from an opposing player. If a foul is committed, the other team is entitled to a *free throw* at the basket. Holding the ball and pushing another player are fouls. So are body-blocking (stopping another player with your body) and tripping. A player who is fouled may be awarded one or more free throws.

Scoring

A basket made during play is called a *field goal*. It adds two points to the team's score. In professional games, a field goal scored more than 23 feet 9 inches (7.2 m) from the basket (19 feet 9 inches [6 m] in college and high school) counts three points. A goal scored by a free throw counts one point. Free throws

are taken from the *free throw line*, 15 feet (4.6 m) from the basket. The game is a *tie* if both teams finish with the same score. The teams must then play one or more *overtime* periods to break the tie. Overtime periods last for five minutes, except in high school games, when overtime periods last for three minutes.

High school basketball games are divided into four *quarters*. Each quarter lasts eight minutes. There is a one-minute break between quarters. The players get a ten-minute rest, called the *half*, after the first two quarters. College games have two 20-minute halves (periods). Professional games are the longest with four 12-minute quarters.

Practice and Fun

Height is not too important for young basketball players. But it is a big factor in college and Olympic basketball. And almost all professional basketball players are extremely tall.

The tallest player has some advantage. A tall center can easily get the jump ball when the referee starts the game. A tall player does not have to reach so high to pop the ball into the basket. If you are tall, you can outreach an opposing player by stretching your arms over your opponent's head. You can catch more high passes. You can also leap up and be the first one to get a *rebound*—when someone shoots, and the ball misses the basket and bounces off the backboard.

Having tall players is not enough to win a basketball game, however. Players must know the rules. They must also know the strategy of the

◄ **Defensive players must be skilled in "blocking" passes or shots. Body contact is not permitted, so anticipating an opponent's move is important.**

COMMON TERMS IN BASKETBALL

Field goal
Making a basket during play. It counts as either two or three points

Foul
An infraction of the rules (illegal physical contact, delay of game, unsportsmanlike conduct)

Free throw
Making a throw after a foul by the opposing team. It counts as one point

Opening tap
The referee throws the ball in the air. Both centers try to tap it to a teammate

Screening
Blocking an opposing player without contact

Dribbling
Bouncing the ball on the floor, using only one hand, in order to take the ball past opposing players and down the court

Traveling
Holding the ball while moving down the court

Rebound
A bounce off the backboard or basket

SOME BASKETBALL RECORDS

Record	Player	Total	Date
Most points scored in one game	Wilt Chamberlain	100	Mar. 2, 1962
Most points scored in one season	Wilt Chamberlain	4,029	1961–1962
Most field goals made in one game	Wilt Chamberlain	36	Mar. 2, 1962
Most free throws made in one game	Wilt Chamberlain	28	Mar. 2, 1962
Most rebounds made in one game	Wilt Chamberlain	55	Nov. 24, 1960
Most games won in a season	Boston Celtics	82	1985–1986
Most NBA championships won	Boston Celtics	16	1957–1986

From 1959 to 1973, Wilt Chamberlain played in the National Basketball Association (NBA) with the Philadelphia Warriors, Philadelphia 76ers, San Francisco Warriors, and Los Angeles Lakers. He held the record for the most points scored by a player in NBA history (31,419), until it was beaten by Kareem Abdul-Jabbar (38,387).

Basketball players wear rubber-soled shoes that lace up over the ankle and give support.

You do not have to be a member of a high school or college team to play basketball. All you need is a ball and a basket. Many families mount a basket on the side of their house, garage, or barn. Playgrounds often have basketball courts. Any small group of people can play this informal type of basketball.

Basketball is played in more than 1,000 colleges and universities in the United States. There are many intercollegiate basketball conferences, such as the Atlantic Coast Conference, the Big Ten, the Big East, the Southeast Conference, and the Ivy League. At the end of the season, many teams participate in holiday tournaments, such as the National Invitational Tournament (NIT), and the National Collegiate Athletic Association (NCAA) championships.

U.S. men professional players compete in the National Basketball Association (NBA), which is divided

game. This means they must study team plans that often help make baskets. They must move quickly. They must be able to catch the ball well. And they must practice making baskets and passing to teammates.

Body contact—like blocking or tackling in football—is not permitted in basketball. Body contact is a foul, so injuries are fairly rare in the sport.

▶ An exciting moment of action as Shaquille ("the Shaq") O'Neal dunks the ball to score a field goal.

WHERE TO DISCOVER MORE

Anderson, Dave. *The Story of Basketball.* New York: Morrow, 1988.

Boyd, Brendan C. *Hoops: Behind the Scenes With the Boston Celtics.* Boston: Little, Brown & Co., Inc., 1989.

into Eastern and Western conferences. In professional basketball, a team loses possession of the ball if it fails to shoot within 24 seconds of taking possession. Under NCAA rules, the offensive team must shoot within 35 seconds of taking the ball.

▶ ▶ ▶ ▶ **FIND OUT MORE** ◀ ◀ ◀ ◀
Sports

BAT

If there were a contest to choose "The Most Remarkable Creature in the World," the bat would have a pretty good chance of winning. Bats look odd, with their mouselike bodies, their big ears, and their strange skin-covered wings. They look even more odd when they sleep. Why? Because they hang upside-down, with their wings draped around their bodies. Scientists find them interesting, because in many ways bats are different from all other animals.

For one thing, the bat is the only mammal that flies. Some other mammals, such as the so-called flying squirrel, can glide in the air. But only the bat can fly like a bird. It flies very well, but most bats need a place to take off from. If you put a bat on the ground, it probably would not be able to fly away. It must climb onto something high, like a tree limb or a rock ledge, in order to launch itself into the air. In fact, most bats would be quite helpless on the ground. Their legs are so weak that they can hardly walk.

Unlike the wings of birds and insects, the bat's wings are made of skin. It has short front legs, or arms, and large "hands" with thin bony fingers. The fingers are longer than the bat's whole body. They are covered with a tough *membrane* (a thin sheet of skin) that stretches all the way down to the bat's ankles. There is also a smaller membrane between the bat's feet.

Bats can fly in total darkness and yet never bump into anything! This is because the bat has a built-in "radar system." As it flies, the bat utters a series of cries that are so high-pitched a person cannot hear them. The sound waves from these cries bounce off objects and echo back to the bat's ears. From these echoes, the bat can tell where the objects are. An old superstition says that bats often try to get caught in the long hair of women. This is untrue. The bat is not at all interested in getting tangled in hair. Its radar system helps it to avoid people's heads as well as other obstacles in its path. It is also not true that bats are blind. They do depend mainly on their ears, but most of them can see in daylight.

Bats All Over the World
Scientists have discovered and named over 1,200 different species of bats. They are found all over the world, except in the freezing polar regions.

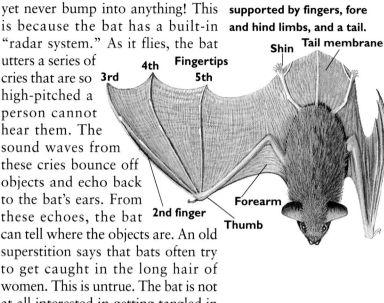

▼ A bat's wings are supported by fingers, fore and hind limbs, and a tail.

Shin · Tail membrane · 4th · Fingertips · 3rd · 5th · 2nd finger · Forearm · Thumb

▼ How "bat radar" works. A bat makes a high-pitched sound while flying. The sound bounces off objects, such as a moth, in the form of echoes. These echoes give the bat information about the direction and distance of objects. The moth in this picture escapes from the bat.

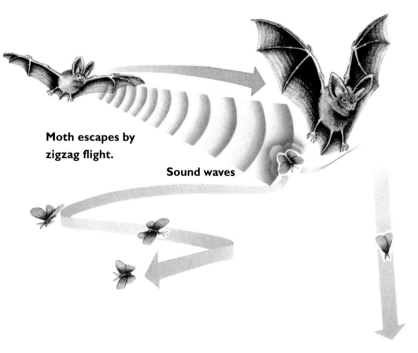

Moth escapes by zigzag flight.

Sound waves

▼ Four American bats. The Mexican freetail bat lives in big colonies. The other three species, however, roost singly or in small colonies. Big brown bats are occasionally seen flying during the day. They feed on insects.

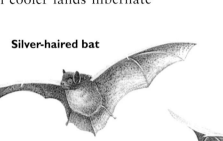

Mexican freetail bat

Silver-haired bat

Long-eared myotis

Big brown bat

▼ The fruit bat's face resembles that of a fox. It is often called a "flying fox."

▶ This early battery was invented by the Italian scientist Alessandro Volta in 1800.

But people hardly ever see them, because they are creatures of the night. During the day they sleep in caves, in trees, or even in houses. Most bats live in hot climates. Those that live in cooler lands hibernate during the winter, or migrate to warmer places.

Most bats are *insect-eaters*. They snatch their meals while flying. Sometimes, instead of using its mouth, a bat will scoop up a flying bug with its wings or with the basket formed by the webbing between its feet. Other bats are *fruit-eaters*. But many also eat meat, fish, or nectar from flowers. One kind of bat with unusual eating habits is the sharp-toothed *vampire bat* of Central and South America. It nips the skin of a sleeping animal and then laps up the blood. The victim doesn't even wake up, because the nip doesn't hurt at all. These bats are dangerous to humans only if they carry the disease rabies. Other kinds of bats do not harm people, although fruit-eaters may damage a farmer's orchard. The insect-eaters are helpful, because they feed on harmful insects such as mosquitoes, and fruit-eating insects.

The *red bat* of the United States and Mexico gives birth to three or four young at a time. The little fruit-eating *brown bat* is the common cave-dwelling bat of North America. It is only 4 inches (10 cm) long, but its wings spread to 10 inches (25 cm). The largest bat is the so-called *flying fox* of Asia and the Pacific Islands. This tree-dwelling bat can have wings as long as 5 feet (152 cm).

▶▶▶▶ **FIND OUT MORE** ◀◀◀◀
Flying Mammal; Mammal; Radar

☼ BATTERY

A battery is a device that produces electricity. It contains special chemicals that change into other chemicals as it works.

The most common kind of battery is the battery that you put into a machine such as a calculator, digital watch, tape player, or flashlight. It has a zinc case with a cap at each end. The two caps are the *terminals* of the battery. One is labeled + (plus, or positive); the other − (minus, or negative). When properly in place, the terminals press against metal contacts that are connected to a switch in the machine. Pressing the switch

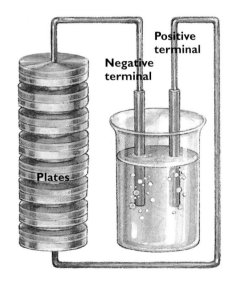

Positive terminal

Negative terminal

Plates

completes the electrical circuit and electricity flows from the plus terminal through the machine and back to the minus terminal.

Inside the case of this kind of battery is a mixture of chemicals and a central rod. The chemicals react together. They change into other chemicals, releasing particles of electricity called *electrons* that move to the rod.

When the machine is switched on, the electrons flow from the rod into the machine and back to the case. These moving electrons make up an electric current. The electron flow stops as soon as the machine is switched off or the battery is taken out. But when all the chemicals inside have changed, no more electrons are produced and the battery is dead.

A battery with a single case is called a *cell*. An automobile battery usually contains six 2-volt cells connected together to give 12 volts of electricity. It can be recharged with electricity and used again. Feeding a direct current into the battery changes the chemicals formed back into the original chemicals.

LEARN BY DOING

You can make a simple battery out of a lemon. You need a brass thumbtack, a paper clip, a flashlight bulb (of less than 3 volts), electrical wire, and a lemon. Stick the pin and paper clip into opposite sides of a fresh lemon. Connect the flashlight bulb to the pin and paper clip with two pieces of electrical wire. The bulb should light up. The pin and the clip act as the terminals. The acidic lemon juice is the chemical that makes electricity.

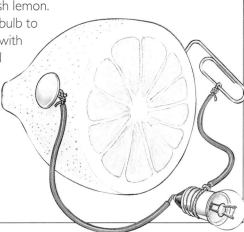

▼ Dry batteries are useful for supplying small quantities of electricity for devices such as flashlights and calculators. A pastelike chemical mixture is packed around a carbon rod inside the dry battery. When the chemicals are used up, the battery cannot be recharged. A wet battery, such as a car battery, contains chemicals that do not get used up. When the battery has run down, it can be recharged by connecting it to an outside electric current.

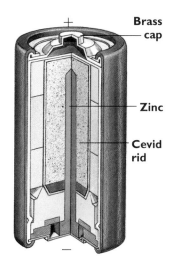

Brass cap

Zinc

Cevid rid

DRY BATTERY

FLASHLIGHT

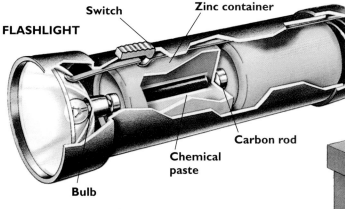

Switch

Zinc container

Carbon rod

Chemical paste

Bulb

Batteries, even small ones, should be handled with care. Dispose of a battery if there is any leakage of chemicals visible on the case. An automobile battery should be handled only by an adult—*never* touch the chemicals inside it.

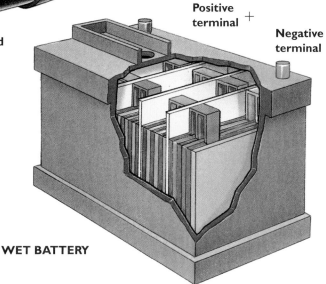

Positive terminal +

Negative terminal −

WET BATTERY

▶▶▶▶ **FIND OUT MORE** ◀◀◀◀
Electricity

BATTLES, FAMOUS

Wars have played an important part in the history of the world. Certain battles that were not really very important have become important to the countries that fought them. The first battles of the Revolutionary War took place at the towns of Lexington and Concord in Massachusetts. Nothing was really decided by these battles, but Americans often call the first shot fired the "shot heard 'round the world." It was not until two years later, when the Americans won the Battle of Saratoga, that the new nation was taken seriously.

Some battles, however, have been "turning points"—they have changed world history. For example, the Persian army of King Darius I tried to conquer Greece in 490 B.C. The Athenian army of 10,000 men, under General Miltiades, met 30,000 Persians at Marathon, a plain 25 miles (40 km) from Athens. Almost 5,000 Persians were killed in the bloody battle. Fewer than 200 Greeks died, and their graves still stand on the battlefield. The Greeks won the battle and the Persians sailed away. Legend says that Miltiades was afraid they would attack Athens before the city learned of his victory. He sent Pheidippides, the army's fastest runner, to carry the news back to the city. Pheidippides ran swiftly back to the city, said "Rejoice, we conquer!" and then collapsed and died. This is why we call a long-distance race a marathon. The Persians, tired and hurt, did not attack Athens. The Battle of Marathon was one of history's turning points. By stopping the Persian invasion, it left Greece free to develop into a great civilization. Read more about the other turning points shown in the table on the opposite page.

▼ The battle of Salamis was fought in 480 B.C. between the Greek and Persian navies. The Greeks had swift ships, called *triremes*, which drove the Persians into a confused huddle. The triremes had about 70 oars grouped in threes on either side of the ship.

FAMOUS BATTLES

Battle	Date	Who Fought	Why Decisive
Salamis (Aegean Sea)	480 B.C.	Greek and Persian navies	The Persians might have conquered much of Europe if the Greeks had not destroyed half their fleet.
Arbela (modern Iraq)	331 B.C.	Alexander the Great and Darius III	The armies of Alexander the Great defeated the armies of Darius III. Alexander then conquered Persia.
Zama (North Africa)	202 B.C.	Rome and Carthage	The Roman general Scipio defeated Carthage's troops, led by Hannibal. The defeat of Carthage led to the domination of the Mediterranean by the Romans.
Tours (France)	A.D. 732	The Franks and the Moors	Charles Martel, ruler of the Franks, defeated the Moors. This battle stopped the Muslim invasion of Europe.
Hastings (England)	1066	England and France	William the Conqueror, Duke of Normandy, defeated Harold, King of England. Harold was killed and the Normans became rulers of England.
Orléans (France)	1429	France and England	Joan of Arc and her French soldiers drove the English out of Orléans. Her victory helped free France of the English invaders.
Lepanto (Mediterranean)	1571	Allied Christians Turkey	Allied fleet of galleys under Don John of Austria defeated the Turkish fleet, weakening the Ottoman Empire.
Defeat of the Spanish Armada	1588	England and Spain	Philip II of Spain sent a huge armada of ships to invade England. The English navy and savage storms defeated the armada and Spain lost control of the seas.
Blenheim (Bavaria)	1704	Britain and Austria against France and Bavaria	Allied British and Austrian armies defeated French and Bavarians. Vienna was saved. Territorial expansion of King Louis XIV of France was stopped.
Quebec (Canada)	1759	Britain and France	General James Wolfe defeated French led by the Marquis de Montcalm. Both generals died in this battle of the French and Indian War on the Plains of Abraham outside the city of Quebec. France driven out of Canada.
Saratoga (New York)	1777	America and Britain	British troops under General Burgoyne surrendered to American General Gates. It was the turning point of the Revolutionary War.
Yorktown (Virginia)	1781	America and France against Britain	George Washington's troops, with French help, defeat the British led by Charles Cornwallis. The surrender led to the end of the Revolutionary War in America.
Waterloo (Belgium)	1815	Britain, Prussia,- Belgium, Netherlands against France.	Soldiers of Britain, Prussia, and the Netherlands crushed the army of Napoleon I of France. Napoleon's plan to regain power in Europe was ended.
Gettysburg (Pennsylvania)	1863	Union Army and Confederate Army	Union armies defeated Confederate armies in one of the bloodiest battles of the Civil War. This battle was a turning point of the war.
Sedan (France)	1870	Germany and France	The German army invaded France and defeated Emperor Napoleon III. This victory marked the rise of a strong and united Germany.
Marne (France)	1914	France and Germany	The French army stopped a wide German advance at the start of World War I. The Germans lost the chance for a quick victory.
Midway Island (Pacific Ocean)	1942	United States and Japan	This air and naval battle stopped Japan's drive across the Pacific. The United States gained time to build ships and aircraft to defeat Japan in World War II.
Normandy (France)	1944	U.S., France, Britain against Germany	General Dwight D. Eisenhower led an army of three million on "D-day" to free Europe from German control. This led to Germany's defeat.
Dien Bien Phu (North Vietnam)	1954	France against Viet Minh forces	The French fought a disastrous war and suffered defeat, accepted an armistice, and the Communists gained control of North Vietnam under the leadership of Ho Chi Minh.

▲ **L. Frank Baum, American writer of children's stories.**

BAUM, L. FRANK (1856–1919)

Frank Baum, the author of *The Wonderful Wizard of Oz*, was born in Chittenango, New York. He began writing for a newspaper. His first book was *Mother Goose in Prose*, in 1897. Baum wrote his first *Wizard of Oz* book in 1900.

Baum moved to California, where he lived and worked for the rest of his life. He used several *pen names* (names other than his own), and he wrote more than 30 books for boys and girls. But the 14 books about the land of Oz are his most famous.

The Wonderful Wizard of Oz tells the story of Dorothy, a little girl from Kansas. She is blown away by a cyclone. Dorothy and her dog, Toto, land in the magical land of Oz. To get home, Dorothy must find the Wizard of Oz, who lives in the Emerald City. The Tin Woodman, the Cowardly Lion, and the Scarecrow join Dorothy in her search.

▶▶▶▶ **FIND OUT MORE** ◀◀◀◀
Children's Literature

BAY

SEE SEACOAST

BEACH

SEE SEACOAST

BEAN

Beans are very good for you. They are among the most nutritious vegetables that people eat regularly. Many types of beans are high in protein, carbohydrates, and vitamins. Farmers like to plant beans because they enrich the soil with *nitrogen*.

Beans are the nutritious seeds and pods of certain plants in the *legume* family. They are related to peas. Like peas, beans have seeds that grow in long shells called *pods*. Bean plants grow quickly and produce a nourishing yield within two months. Some bean plants are bushy and grow low to the ground. Others, known as *climbing beans*, or *pole beans*, twine themselves around poles, strings, or the branches of other plants.

Kidney beans are the most important type of bean grown in the United States. Chili con carne uses red kidney beans. The *dry beans* that we use for some meals are seeds that have ripened and hardened. They are rich in protein and can be used as substitutes for meat.

Other types of kidney beans can be eaten before the seeds ripen. *String beans* and *snap beans* are picked young, when the seeds are still tender. People eat the shells as well as the seeds of these beans. These *green shell beans* are rich in vitamins A, B, and C.

Kidney beans are grown around the world but were first cultivated by the Aztecs and other Native Americans of Central and South America. Like other "New World" crops, such as potatoes and tomatoes, they were introduced to Europe by the first explorers in America.

Other types of beans are also important. *Soybeans* are rich in protein and are also grown to enrich the soil. *Mung beans*, originally from Asia, can be eaten fresh or cooked. Beansprouts usually come from mung beans.

▶▶▶▶ **FIND OUT MORE** ◀◀◀◀
Carbohydrates; Food; Protein; Vegetables; Vitamins and Minerals

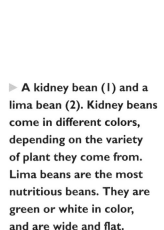

▶ **A kidney bean (1) and a lima bean (2). Kidney beans come in different colors, depending on the variety of plant they come from. Lima beans are the most nutritious beans. They are green or white in color, and are wide and flat.**

1

2

BEAR

A fat body curled into a ball for a long winter's nap. A pair of playful cubs scrambling up a tree. An angry mother fiercely defending her young. This may be how you think of the large, furry mammals called bears.

Bears look friendly. But they are large, powerful animals. They can be dangerous. You may have heard of hikers in Yellowstone National Park who were horribly injured or even killed by bears. Most bears will attack only if teased or threatened in some way. But all bears, especially the big grizzly, can be dangerous. Never approach a bear and *never* feed or tease one.

The bear is a heavily built animal. Unlike most mammals, it walks with the soles of its feet flat on the ground. This lumbering gait makes bears seem clumsy. But bears can be good runners. Most are also excellent swimmers and climbers. A bear can even take a few steps upright, on its hind legs.

Bears belong to the animal group called *carnivores* (meat-eaters). The larger bears kill and eat animals such as deer or seals. Fish is a favorite food, and bears also eat small creatures such as frogs, mice, and grubs. But they are also very fond of plant roots, berries, and nuts. Honey is a special favorite for bears.

Bears usually live alone. They have poor eyesight, but keen senses of smell and hearing. Those that live in cold northern lands retire to caves during the worst months of the winter. But they do not sleep soundly

the whole time, as true hibernating animals do. A loud sound can easily awaken a bear. On warm winter days, a bear may awaken and leave its cave for a short time. Toward the end of the winter, the female bear gives birth to her *cubs* in the cave. Most often, there are two babies, although some times there may be as many as four.

The *brown bears* of North America, Europe, and Asia are among the largest carnivores in the world. They may be up to 9 feet (2.7 m) long and weigh over 1,500 pounds (680 kg). Brown bears include the *Alaskan bear* and the *Kodiak*, which lives on Kodiak Island off Alaska. In spite of their name, brown bears are not always brown. They may be yellowish, black, or tan.

The *grizzly* is one of the best-known brown bears. It may be as much as 8 feet (2.4 m) long and weigh up to 800 pounds (362 kg). Because they are so big and heavy, full-grown grizzlies never climb trees. At one time there were large numbers of these powerful giants in the western United States. But now they are rare, because so many have been shot by hunters. Today, there are only about 1,000 grizzlies, some 200 of which are living in the safety of Yellowstone National Park.

The smaller *black bears* are also found in national parks. They often seem quite tame. A black bear may rush right over to a car stopped on the road and stand with its front paws against the window, waiting to be given a snack. But people should

▲ A black bear cub. The black bear is the most common species of bear found in North America.

▼ Bears of North America. Although the grizzly bear is fiercer, it is not as large as the Alaskan brown bear, which grows up to 9 feet (2.7 m) long and is the largest bear in the world and the largest land carnivore.

Grizzly bear

Polar bear

Black bear

Brown bear

never feed or try to pet these animals. Even a friendly one can suddenly become very dangerous. Other black bears inhabit forests in Asia.

The *polar bear* of the icy North Pole has a heavy white coat that keeps it warm in the freezing cold. Fur on the bottom of its feet keeps it from slipping on the ice. Seals, seabirds, fish, and reindeer make up the polar bear's main food. But it also enjoys summer leaves and berries. The polar bear is an excellent swimmer and often travels great distances on floating ice floes.

The small *spectacled bear* of South America is only about 2 feet (61 cm) high at the shoulder. It has black and brown hair with lighter circles around the eyes, which make the bear look as if it were wearing spectacles (glasses). The *Malayan sun bear* of east Asia is a small tree-living bear with orangy-white, ring-shaped marks on the chest. An unusual bear is the *sloth bear* of India. Its snout is long and pointed like an anteater's. Its body is covered with long, shaggy hair, and it has a V-shaped mark on its chest. With its long curved claws, the sloth bear digs termites from their nests. The claws also help the bear climb trees in search of fruit or honey.

Probably everyone has heard of Smokey the Bear. Most people know him as a cartoon character on posters that teach people how to prevent forest fires. But the cartoon was based on a real black bear that had been rescued from a fire. Smokey lived for many years in the National Zoo in Washington, D.C.

▶ ▶ ▶ **FIND OUT MORE** ◀ ◀ ◀
Carnivore; Hibernation; Mammal; Panda; Polar Life

BEAUFORT SCALE

SEE WIND

BEAVER

A person who works very hard is often described as an "eager beaver" or a "busy beaver." In fact, the beaver is a creature of amazing skill and energy. It works constantly at building and repairing its home and getting food.

This large rodent is much more at home in the water than on land. Its plump body, about 2 to 3 feet (60 to 90 cm) long, is covered with coarse brown hair. It has a flat, scaly tail that looks like a paddle. The front feet have sharp claws for digging and carrying, and the hind feet are webbed for swimming. The beaver can hold its breath under water for as long as 15 minutes. Its large, sharp teeth are used to gnaw tender tree bark, the beaver's favorite food. The teeth are also used in felling trees and cutting logs and twigs for use as building materials.

Beavers live and work together in family groups. A pond with a good supply of willow, poplar, and birch trees is the perfect spot for a beaver colony to set up housekeeping. The

▼ A beaver keeps its long front teeth sharp by constant gnawing on branches and trunks of trees.

▼ A beaver's lodge has underwater entrances. The lodge is built of sticks, branches, grass, and mud.

beavers build their home, called a *lodge,* using sticks and mud. The door to the lodge is under the water, but the living space inside, which is lined with dry earth and leaves, is above water. Beavers often build dams across streams and small rivers to keep the water of the pond at a constant level. Trees are felled at the water's edge and then gnawed into logs. The beavers carry or drag the logs into the water and float them into place. Then they plaster the logs together with mud to secure the dam.

There are some beavers in Europe, but there are more beavers in North America than anywhere else in the world. The American beaver has long been hunted for its thick, velvety, waterproof fur. Early settlers also killed beavers for their meat. Beavers can be a pest, but in many places these busy animals are now protected by American and Canadian law.

The rodent called the *mountain beaver* or *sewellel* of the West is not closely related to the beaver. It is only about 12 inches (30 cm) long, has no tail, and looks more like a muskrat than a beaver.

▷▷▷▷ **FIND OUT MORE** ◁◁◁◁
Fur; Rodent

BECKET, THOMAS A (1118–1170)

The churchman, Thomas à Becket, played an important part in the conflict between Church and king in England during the 1100s. At first, Becket was a faithful servant of the state. He won the friendship of the young king, Henry II, who made him *chancellor* (chief justice) of England in 1155. Becket lived a life of wealth and ease at this time. But after becoming Archbishop of Canterbury in 1162, he gave up his luxuries and devoted himself wholeheartedly to the Church. From this time on, he

and the king began to quarrel bitterly over certain rights of the Church.

During the Middle Ages, priests who committed crimes were tried by the Church, not by the king's courts. Henry wanted to pass a law to make the clergy subject to royal law. But Becket upheld the rights of the Church. He also resisted Henry's efforts to tax the Church. The quarrel between the two became so seri-

▲ The murder of Thomas à Becket in Canterbury Cathedral, 1170.

ous that Becket had to flee to France for a while. He made the king even more furious after returning to England in 1170. He asked the pope to *excommunicate* (cast out of the Church) the bishops who supported the king's demands. It is said that Henry exclaimed, "Is there no one who will rid me of this turbulent priest?" Four noblemen took him at his word. They went to Canterbury Cathedral on December 29, 1170, and murdered Becket on his way to evening prayers. Pope Alexander III declared Thomas à Becket a saint less than three years after his murder.

▷▷▷▷ **FIND OUT MORE** ◁◁◁◁
English History; Henry, Kings of England

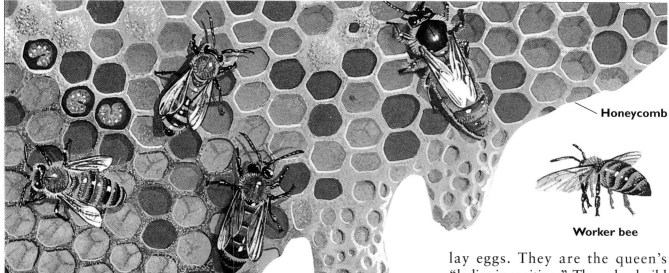

Honeycomb

Worker bee

Cell with honey inside

Royal cell

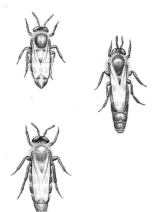

▲ A close-up view of a honeybee comb. The comb is made of wax. Each six-sided cell serves either as a nursery or as a storage for food. The workers feed pollen or honey to growing larvae while new queens in the "royal cells" are fed special food.

BEDOUIN

SEE NOMAD

BEE

A busy honeybee is one of our best friends. Without it, we would have no honey or beeswax. We could probably not even enjoy such fruits as apples, peaches, and plums. Honeybees carry *pollen* (the yellow powder found in flowers) from one blossom to another. In this way the plants are fertilized so they can grow seeds for a new generation of plants.

Life in a Honeybee Colony

Honeybees are like people; they are *social* animals that live and work together in groups, or *colonies*. Life in a honeybee hive is nearly as complicated as life in a city. In each colony, there are three classes of bees: a *queen, workers,* and *drones.* The queen is larger than the other bees. Her job is to lay eggs. The drones are males whose only task is to mate with the queen. Soon after they have done their duty, they die. The busy workers are females, but they cannot make or

lay eggs. They are the queen's "ladies-in-waiting." They also build the hive, gather food, make honey, and care for the young.

Inside the hive is a marvelous structure called a *honeycomb*. It is made of wax, produced from the workers' bodies. The honeycomb is made up of many six-sided "cubbyholes" called *cells*. Some cells are used as storage bins for honey and pollen, which the bees eat. The workers collect pollen in little "baskets" formed by the hair on their hind legs. The honey they make comes from *nectar*, a sweet fluid found in flowers. Each worker gathers nectar with her long tongue and stores it in a special part of her body called the *honey stomach*. She puts the nectar into the cells. Special chemicals that come from the honey stomach turn the nectar into honey. A worker can tell other workers in the hive where a good supply of nectar and pollen can be found. She does this by special kinds of movements called *dances*.

The queen lays her eggs in other cells of the honeycomb. A bee egg is even smaller than the period at the end of this sentence. But each egg hatches into a wormlike *larva*, which grows quickly. At first, the larvae are fed *royal jelly*, a food that comes from the glands in the workers' heads. After a few days, most of the larvae are given *beebread*, a mixture of honey and pollen. But those larvae that are to become new queens are fed only with royal jelly. Each larva becomes a *pupa*. Finally, after 12 days, the pupa becomes an adult.

The body of the adult honeybee has three parts—head, thorax, and abdomen. Two *antennae*, or feelers, are attached to the front of the head. They are used for smelling as well as feeling. The bee's tongue is a long hairy tube used for sucking water, honey, and nectar. The bee's jaws are used for grasping pollen and wax.

The *thorax* supports the bee's six legs and its two pairs of wings. The *abdomen* is the rear part of the body. The worker's abdomen carries a straight *stinger* covered with pointed barbs. Usually the honeybee will only sting in self-defense. When it does, the barbs stick into the flesh of the victim. After losing its stinger the bee dies. The queen has a smooth, curved stinger, which she uses only for fighting with rival queens. The drone has no stinger at all.

Some people keep honeybees as a hobby. Others raise bees in order to sell the honey and wax that they make. Honey is used in baking, as a sweetener, and as a spread. Wax is made into useful objects such as candles. The beekeeper has a special shed called an *apiary*. Inside, the bees are housed in manmade hives.

Other Kinds of Bees

Besides honeybees, there are other species of bees. Like the honeybee, the large black-and-yellow *bumblebee* and the *stingless bee* are social insects. Bumblebees are helpful to farmers because they pollinate red clover plants. They also make honey, but it is not used by people. The stingless bees actually do have stingers, but they do not use them. Instead, they defend themselves by biting with their jaws. These bees are found only in tropical parts of the world.

The carpenter, leafcutter, miner, and mason bees are *solitary* insects.

They live alone, not in colonies. The *carpenter bee* builds its nest in the twigs or branches of a dead tree. The *leafcutter bee* tunnels in the ground or in soft wood and makes its home with leaves. Eggs are laid in little cups formed by the leaves. *Miner bees* live in underground tunnels. The *mason bee* nests in rotten wood or in an empty snail shell. The *guest* or *cuckoo bee* leaves its eggs in the nest of other bees to be cared for.

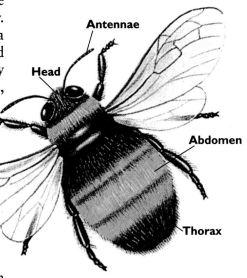

Head

Antennae

Abdomen

Thorax

▶ ▶ ▶ ▶ **FIND OUT MORE** ◀ ◀ ◀ ◀
Insect; Metamorphosis; Wasps and Hornets

BEER

SEE FERMENTATION

BEETHOVEN, LUDWIG VAN (1770–1827)

Beethoven is one of the world's great composers and an important figure in the history of music. He developed new musical forms and he greatly enlarged the repertory for orchestra, piano, voice, and other instruments. He took harmony beyond the harmony of Bach and Mozart. He helped start a whole new kind of music, which came to be known as the *Romantic* style.

▲ When a honeybee finds flowers rich in nectar, it returns to the hive and does a figure 8 dance on the honeycomb. The movements and the position of the figure 8 in this dance tell other workers where the food is.

▲ Most bees sting only in defense. The stinger has a barbed tip. After using it, the bee dies. Some bees, such as the African *killer bee*, are more aggressive and will sting more readily.

Beethoven was born in Bonn, Germany. His father was a poor court musician. When Ludwig was 5 he began to study the violin, and soon after, he took up other instruments. By the time he was 10, Ludwig was composing his own music. He got his first job as an organ player at 12. Four of his compositions were published that same year.

Ludwig grew into a sensitive, moody young music teacher with poor manners and a quick temper. But he was generous and warm-hearted. He made and kept many important friends who forgave his faults. He dedicated many of his compositions to them.

He moved to Vienna, Austria, in 1792 and for a time studied with the famous composer Franz Joseph Haydn. Beethoven stayed in Austria for the rest of his life. Unlike other composers who had rich *patrons,* or backers, Beethoven worked alone, a free spirit. He composed symphonies, sonatas, chorales, concertos, quartets, overtures, opera, and much more. His nine symphonies, however, tower over all his other compositions.

At the age of 27, Beethoven discovered that he was losing his hearing. This was a terrible thing for a musical genius. Beethoven kept his deafness secret for a long time. He finally became almost totally deaf, and was able to hear his last great works only in his imagination as he put the notes on paper.

▶▶▶▶ **FIND OUT MORE** ◀◀◀◀
Choral Music; Music; Romantic Period

▲ **A bronze bust of Ludwig van Beethoven. He is one of the most popular and influential composers in the history of Western music. His works remain among the most often performed pieces of music ever written.**

▶ **Dung beetles, as the name suggests, feed on dung. They clear away dung by rolling it into a ball and then bury it in the soil. This is a useful process, because nutrients in the dung are put back into the soil and recycled.**

BEETLE

Did you ever see a purple tiger? There is such a creature—but it is not really a tiger. It is a small, fierce beetle. This tiger beetle attacks other insects with its jaws.

Perhaps you are more familiar with the ladybug, the firefly, and the weevil. These and thousands of other beetles belong to one of the largest groups of insects. Like the purple tiger, all are good biters, for they have strong jaws, called *mandibles.* Like other insects, they also have three pairs of legs and a pair of feelers. Nearly all beetles have two hard outer front wings, which cover a delicate pair of back wings. Only the back wings are used for flying.

The plump body of a beetle is protected by a brittle, horny shell. The hard front wings form part of this shell. You sometimes find the hard shell of a dead beetle. It breaks with a crunching sound. This shell, like the bones in your body, is the beetle's skeleton. It is an outside skeleton, or *exoskeleton.* While many beetles are harmful pests, others are helpful friends because they kill insects that are pests. The polka-dotted ladybug (also called a ladybird) eats aphids and other plant-harming bugs. And some perfectly harmless beetles are colorful creatures that are fun to watch as they crawl or fly around.

Beetle Types
Beetles vary in many other ways as well. One of these ways is size. The striped and spotted *Goliath beetle* of Africa is bigger than

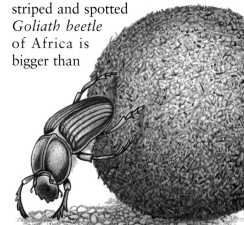

a mouse, while the lovely ladybug is no bigger than a mouse's eye.

Beetles also make their homes in different kinds of places all over the world. They are found under rocks, behind the bark of trees, in and on all kinds of plants, and even in the underground nests of ants or moles.

The tiny, long-snouted *weevil* lives in farmers' storage bins, where it damages wheat and other grains. A living-room rug, unfortunately, may be a cozy home and a tasty meal for

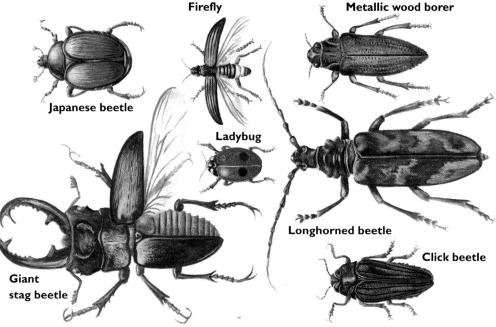

Firefly

Japanese beetle

Ladybug

Metallic wood borer

Longhorned beetle

Click beetle

Giant stag beetle

▲ Not all beetles are pests. In fact, most are useful. The burying beetle is a useful scavenger. It buries the bodies of dead animals as food for its larvae.

◄ Beetles include the most useful and the most destructive of insects. The ladybug, for example, eats garden pests such as aphids. The Japanese beetle, introduced by accident into North America, destroys cultivated plants and fruits.

the young of the *carpet beetle*. These beetles may also be found in closets, happily chewing on woolens or furs. Some beetles live in or on water. The shiny black *whirligig* whirls madly about on the surface of a pond. The *diving beetle* plunges head downward into the water, looking for tadpoles, insects, and little fish to eat.

Many beetles have unusual habits. The yellow-and-black *burying beetle* buries the dead bodies of small animals. It lays its eggs in the bodies. The *click beetle* is amusing. If you put one on its back, it rights itself with a clicking sound. However, the young of the click beetle are harmful to trees and wooden furniture. The *museum beetle* creeps into the glass

LEARN BY DOING

You can easily study the life cycle of one kind of beetle, the *mealworm,* and have a constant supply of amphibian or reptilian pet food, too. Buy *mealworm* larvae at a pet store. Put a few of these wormlike animals in a dry fish tank, along with some dry bran, as food for the young, and some pieces of raw potato, the food for the adults. Sprinkle the bran with water now and then, but don't make it or the mealworms soggy.

The larvae will grow about 1 1/4 inches (3 cm) long. Then they become pupas. The pupas do not eat or move about, but their bodies change. Finally, the pupas become adult beetles. The adults lay small oval-shaped eggs from which new larvae hatch. The cycle begins again. How alike, or different, are the larvae, pupas, and adults? How long are newly hatched larvae? Do the larvae or the adults eat more?

▲ **A weevil is a kind of beetle with a long snout or beak. For this reason it is called a *snout beetle*. Weevils do widespread damage to cotton and food plants.**

▼ **In the spring of 1989, student demonstrators gathered in Tianamen Square, Beijing, to call for freedom and democracy. The government sent in troops and tanks to crush the protests.**

cases in museums and munches its way through the bodies of stuffed animals. One of the most fascinating beetles of all is the *firefly*, or *lightning bug,* which is often seen flashing in the darkness of a warm summer night. Parts of its body contain chemicals that produce light that blinks on and off. The beetle uses this light as a signal to attract a mate.

▶▶▶ **FIND OUT MORE** ◀◀◀◀
Insect; Metamorphosis

BEHAVIOR

SEE HABIT, INTELLIGENCE, LEARNING

BEIJING

Beijing is the capital of China and its second largest city. It is also China's educational, cultural, financial, and transportation center. The city lies on a large plain between the Pei and the Hun rivers in northeastern China. There are about six million people living in Beijing.

There has been a city on the site of Beijing for more than 20 centuries. After the Mongols from central Asia conquered China, their emperor, Kublai Khan, made it his capital and called it Khanbalik. In the 1200s,

Marco Polo, a merchant trader from Venice, Italy, spent many years in the city.

Two series of great Chinese emperors, the Mings and the Manchus, built their palaces in the city and called it *Peking,* meaning "northern capital." General Chiang Kai shek, former leader of Nationalist China, moved his headquarters to the south and, from 1928 to 1949, the city was renamed *Peiping,* or "northern peace." When the Communist Chinese captured mainland China, they restored Peking as the capital.

Beijing is made up of cities within cities, all formerly surrounded by huge mud-brick walls. The heart of old Peking was the *Tatar* or Inner City. Within the Inner City was the *Imperial City,* where the government had its offices and government officials lived. Inside the Imperial City was the famous *Forbidden City,* where the emperor himself lived. Nearly a square mile (2.5 sq. km) in area, it contained the imperial palace and grounds encircled by high, pink-washed walls and a deep canal or moat. There was also a walled city for foreigners in Peking.

Today, tourists can enter the Imperial and Forbidden cities and visit the beautiful temples and palaces. The Temple of Heaven and the summer palace of the Manchu emperors are in the south part of the city. The Communist Chinese have done much to clean up the old city and are constructing new buildings. Beijing industries produce iron and steel, machine tools, petrochemicals, electronic and communications equipment, and textiles.

In 1989, Tiananmen Square in Beijing was the site of a terrible massacre when thousands of pro-democracy demonstrators were killed and injured by Communist government troops.

▶▶▶ **FIND OUT MORE** ◀◀◀◀
China; Polo, Marco

BELARUS

Belarus is a land of hills, forests, lakes, and marshes. It was formerly one of the republics that made up the Soviet Union. Then it was known as Byelorussia. Since late 1991, Belarus has been part of the Commonwealth of Independent States. The people speak Byelorussian, which is very similar to Russian.

Belarus is bordered by Lithuania and Latvia on the north, Russia on the east, Ukraine on the south, and Poland on the west. Belarus has long, cold winters and short, warm summers. The Pripyat Marshes cover an area the size of Massachusetts in southern Belarus. They make the climate of Belarus very damp.

Dense forests cover about one-quarter of the country. Many of the hardwood trees are used in the important timber industry. Logs are floated down many of the large rivers, such as the Dnieper, Dvina, and the Nyoman, that flow through Belarus.

Farms in Belarus produce large harvests of wheat, flax, rye, potatoes, and oats. Under Soviet rule crops were grown on large *collective farms*, where groups of families collected their harvests together. Many farms in Belarus are now returning to traditional, one-family ownership.

Nearly two-thirds of the population of Belarus live in cities. Manufacturing industries are the chief employer. Factories produce textiles, automobiles, and farm machinery. Another industry has developed from peat, one of Belarus's natural resources. Peat is a spongy soil made of partially decayed plants. It can be dried and burned. Much of Belarus's electricity comes from power plants that burn peat.

Landlocked Belarus is located at a crossroads of Eastern Europe. It has been overrun and controlled by other countries many times. For hundreds of years it was part of Lithuania, and known as Byelorussia. Russia gained control in 1795.

The eastern part of Byelorussia became part of the Soviet Union at the time of the *Russian Revolution* of 1917. Western Byelorussia became part of Poland at the same time, as part of the European settlement of World War I. The Soviet Union gained control of western Byelorussia in 1945, after World War II.

By 1991, the Soviet Union was showing signs of unraveling. Byelorussia was one of the Soviet republics that declared its independence. It also changed its name to Belarus to erase the memory of communist rule.

On December 8, 1991, the rulers of Belarus, Russia, and Ukraine agreed to form the Commonwealth of Independent States (C.I.S.) to replace the Soviet Union. They were soon joined by eight of the remaining twelve republics. The Belarus capital, Minsk, was chosen as the capital of the C.I.S.

BELARUS

Capital city
Minsk (1,500,000 people)

Area
80,309 square miles
(208,000 sq. km)

Population
10,200,000 people

Government
Republic

Natural resources
Timber, especially hardwood, peat

Export products
Lumber, textiles, machinery

Unit of Money
Ruble

Official Language
Byelorussian

© 1994 GeoSystems, an R.R. Donnelley & Sons Company

▶ ▶ ▶ ▶ **FIND OUT MORE** ◀ ◀ ◀ ◀
Russian History; Lithuania

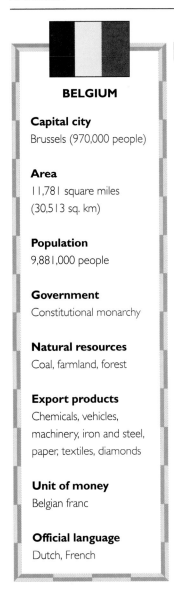

BELGIUM

Capital city
Brussels (970,000 people)

Area
11,781 square miles
(30,513 sq. km)

Population
9,881,000 people

Government
Constitutional monarchy

Natural resources
Coal, farmland, forest

Export products
Chemicals, vehicles,
machinery, iron and steel,
paper, textiles, diamonds

Unit of money
Belgian franc

Official language
Dutch, French

▼ **The headquarters of the European Community are located in this building in Brussels, Belgium.**

BELGIUM

Belgium is a small country in Europe. In the north, 40 miles (64 km) of coastal plain stretches from the Netherlands to France. In the southeast, the Ardennes Forest grows on rocky soil. Belgium is a flat country with numerous cities. (See the map with the article on EUROPE.)

The Belgians are divided into two language groups. The Flemings live in the north and speak a language that is similar to Dutch called Flemish. The people in the south are called Walloons and speak a kind of French called Walloon.

The Belgians are a hard-working people with a long history of skill in business and manufacturing. The cities bustled with craftsmen and merchants even in the Middle Ages. Belgian goods were sold throughout Europe. In the period from the 1400s to the 1600s, Flemish painters perfected the techniques of oil painting.

Because of its location between its larger neighbors, Germany and France, Belgium has often been fought over. Julius Caesar conquered the region for Rome about 50 B.C. He defeated the local people, who were called Belgae. Belgium was ruled by Charlemagne in the late 700s, then by the rulers of Burgundy, Spain, Austria, and France. The French emperor Napoleon suffered his final defeat at Waterloo, a few miles from Brussels, the Belgian capital. Belgium became part of the Netherlands in 1815, after the fall of Napoleon. But the Belgians had little in common with the Dutch. They revolted in 1830 and became an independent nation. Belgium was invaded by the Germans and suffered heavy damage in both the world wars of the 20th century, but it is now prosperous again. Belgium is a constitutional monarchy. The monarch is head of state, but laws are made by parliament. Belgium is mainly a manufacturing country and is a member of the European Community. It has heavy industry (steel and coal) and also makes textiles, lace, machinery,

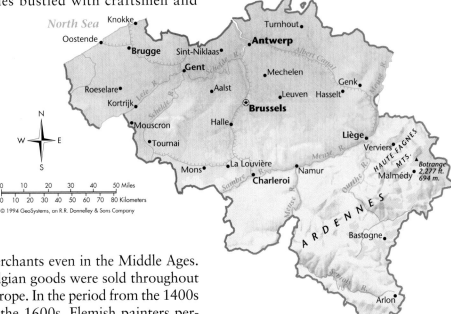

and chocolate. The chief cities are Brussels, Antwerp, Brugge, Gent, and Liège. The Belgians have learned to be efficient farmers, because they have no land to spare. Their main crops are barley, sugar beet, wheat, and potatoes.

▶▶▶▶ **FIND OUT MORE** ◀◀◀◀
Caesar, Julius; Charlemagne; Europe;

European Community; French History; Napoleon Bonaparte; Netherlands; Romance Languages; Waterloo

BELIZE

Belize, formerly called British Honduras, is a country on the east coast of Central America. The land ranges from a flat, marshy coast to heavily forested mountains in the interior. The climate is hot and wet.

Belizeans are descendants of African slaves, Indians, and Europeans. Spanish and English are spoken. Many people cultivate their own small farms and work for lumber companies and plantations.

English buccaneers settled the former capital, Belize City, in the 1600s. Spain later took control and held the territory for 125 years until Britain took it over in 1786. Belize became independent in 1981.

The government consists of a two-

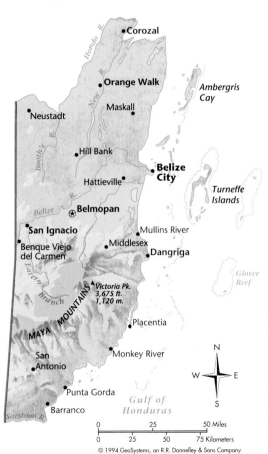

© 1994 GeoSystems, an R.R. Donnelley & Sons Company

house National Assembly and a cabinet headed by a prime minister. Guatemala has long claimed Belize as part of its territory. In 1992, the new Guatemalan president agreed to recognize Belize's political independence, and to try and work out a solution to the territorial problem.

▶▶▶▶ **FIND OUT MORE** ◀◀◀◀
Central America

BELL

Bells can be many different sizes and shapes. They are made of metal, glass, wood, and even clay. All are hollow and are struck to make a tone. A bell may be small enough to hold in your hand or large enough for you to stand inside. The Emperor, or Czar Kolokol Bell in Moscow, Russia, for example, is enormous—it weighs 180 tons (167 metric tons). Whether big or little, most bells are cup-shaped, flaring out at the open end. They may be struck inside by a metal tongue, which is called a *clapper*, or hit on the outside with a hammer.

The earliest bells were wooden. Some were square, instead of round, or beehive-shaped. Ancient peoples learned to make metal bells by pouring hot, melted metal into bell-shaped molds. When the metal cooled, it hardened. Then the mold was removed, and a new bell was finished. This method is still used today.

People began to hang bells in

BELIZE

Capital city
Belmopan (3,500 people)

Area
8,867 square miles
(22,965 sq. km)

Population
190,000 people

Government
Constitutional monarchy

Natural resources
Forest, farmland

Export products
Sugar, bananas, citrus, lumber, chicle, fish

Unit of money
Belize dollar

Official language
English (Spanish is also spoken)

LEARN BY DOING

You can make instruments similar to bells or chimes. Pour water into widemouthed jars. Fill each jar to a different level. Tap the jars gently with a spoon to ring the bells. Use several different sized jars. Can you tune them (by adding water or pouring out water) to play a song?

▲ The giant Emperor Bell in Moscow is the largest in the world. It was cast in 1733 but was cracked by fire in 1737 and since then has never chimed a note.

▼ The telephone was invented by Alexander Graham Bell. In 1892, Bell made a telephone call to Chicago from New York City to demonstrate the usefulness of his new invention to businessmen.

towers long ago and to ring them to tell time, to sound an alarm, and to call people to worship. The bells were rung by hand by pulling long ropes. Today, most bells are rung mechanically. Modern bells—such as chimes and carillons—do not swing as some church bells do but are "hung dead," meaning fixed in place. *Chimes* are small sets of bells tuned to a scale. *Carillons* are large sets, played from a keyboard by a *carillonneur*. The Netherlands Carillon in Arlington, Virginia, has 49 bells.

Bells are part of the *percussion* (musical instrument that must be struck) section in orchestras and bands. A set of hand-rung tuned bells was too awkward to use, so the *glockenspiel*, a set of metal bars struck with a hammer, was developed to give the same sounds. Small bells attached to a strap, called *sleigh bells*, are also used.

▶▶▶▶ **FIND OUT MORE** ◀◀◀◀
Big Ben; Liberty Bell; Music; Percussion Instruments

BELL, ALEXANDER GRAHAM (1847–1922)

On March 10, 1876, Alexander Graham Bell spoke through a strange instrument to his assistant, who was in another room. "Mr. Watson, come here. I want you," Bell said. Thomas Watson heard him and came. That instrument was the first telephone.

Bell was born in Scotland. As he grew up, he learned about voices from his father, who taught the deaf to speak. He was fascinated by the sound of the voice and how the human ear hears it. Bell moved to Canada in 1870 and to Boston in 1871, where he, too, taught the deaf, using a system invented by his father. He later became a United States citizen.

France gave Bell the Volta Prize in 1880 for inventing the telephone. He used the money to set up the Volta

Laboratory to do experiments that might help the deaf. He then organized the Volta Bureau, which also helps the deaf, and he developed several other devices involving sound and hearing. One was the *audiometer*, which measures a person's ability to hear sounds. Another was a machine to record voices, the *phonograph*.

Bell was also interested in working with other scientists. He helped spread scientific knowledge by working with the American Association for the Advancement of Science and the National Geographic Society.

▶▶▶▶ **FIND OUT MORE** ◀◀◀◀
Electricity; Telephone

BELLOW, SAUL (1915–)

One of America's greatest modern writers is Saul Bellow. He was born in Lachine, Quebec, in Canada. His parents had immigrated there from Russia in 1913. When he was 9 years old, the family moved to Chicago. After studying at Chicago and Northwestern universities and graduating in 1937, Saul Bellow began a university teaching career, combined with his life as a writer of novels and stories.

The Bellows were a Jewish family, and Saul grew up fluent in Yiddish, a language that had an influence on his English prose style. He won acclaim in 1953 with *The Adventures of Augie March*, which won the National Book Award for 1954. The heroes of Bellow's books are typically bright, intelligent people trying to succeed in a world where their ideals always seem to be thwarted. His books are full of comedy and shrewd observations of people.

Among Saul Bellow's novels are *Henderson the Rain King*, *Herzog*, *Mr. Sammler's Planet*, and *Humboldt's Gift* (for which he was awarded the Pulitzer Prize in 1976). He won the Nobel Prize for literature in 1976.

BENIN

Benin, formerly called Dahomey, is a West African republic somewhat smaller than Pennsylvania. It became part of French West Africa in the 1890s, and was granted its independence in 1960. It took the name Benin in 1975.

Benin is shaped like a long, narrow rectangle, bounded by Nigeria on the east, Burkina Faso and Niger on the north, Togo on the west, and the Gulf of Guinea on the south.

The coast is flat and sandy. A region of lakes and rivers lies inland. Beyond this area is a vast plateau rising to 1,500 feet (457 m). The Atakora mountain range lies in the northwest. The Ouémé River,

Bight of Benin

the nation's longest, and the Mono flow southward into the Gulf. The Mékrou and Alibori rivers in the north flow into the Niger River.

Southern Benin is hot and humid, having two rainy seasons a year and two dry ones. The north, however, has two seasons: one wet, one dry.

From about 1500 to 1650, the region was part of the African kingdom of Benin, famous for its ivory and bronze sculpture. The kingdom of Abomey (later Dahomey) ruled until the late 1900s. After independence and several revolutions, a one-party, socialist government took power in 1972, and held office through the 1980s. This ended in 1991 with the formation of an opposition party and the election of a new president.

▶ ▶ ▶ ▶ **FIND OUT MORE** ◀ ◀ ◀ ◀
Africa

BEOWULF

Beowulf is the hero of the epic named after him. An *epic* is a poem that tells the story of a hero. The story came from a combination of Scandinavian history, folktales, and mythology, and is set in Sweden and Denmark. Beowulf was a Swedish prince who set out to save the Danes from the monster, Grendel. After a fierce struggle, he killed the monster. But Grendel's mother, another monster, attacked the Danes. Beowulf killed her, too, and later became king.

The poem is the most important writing in *Anglo-Saxon*, also called *Old English*, the language spoken in England more than 1,000 years ago. The oldest version of the poem that still exists was probably copied about A.D. 1000 by monks. It is in the British Museum. *Beowulf* may have been first written about A.D. 700.

▶ ▶ ▶ ▶ **FIND OUT MORE** ◀ ◀ ◀ ◀
Anglo-Saxons; Folklore; Legend;
Literature; Mythology; Poetry

BENIN

Capital city
Porto-Novo (208,000 people)

Area
43,484 square miles
(112,600 sq. km)

Population
4,741,000 people

Government
Multi-party republic

Natural resources
Oil, forests, hydroelectric power

Export products
Petroleum products, cocoa, cotton, palm oil

Unit of money
Franc

Official language
French

▼ **A bronze mask from Benin. Benin gets its name from a West African empire (at its height in the 1400s) famous for its metalworking.**

The Bering Strait separating Siberia from Alaska is only 51 miles (82 km) wide. In this channel are two small granite-domed islands, only about a mile (1.6 km) apart. One island is part of Siberia, the other belongs to the United States. The International Date Line runs between them.

▲ A map showing the location of the Bering Sea and Bering Strait.

▼ Berlin, Germany's largest city and capital, is a thriving cultural and industrial center.

BERING, VITUS (1681–1741)

A sea, an island, and a *strait* (a water passage), all in the Arctic, are named for Vitus Bering, a Danish explorer. Bering joined the Russian navy when he was a young man. Peter the Great, the Russian czar (emperor), sent Bering on an expedition to the northern Pacific Ocean.

Bering explored the icy waters east of Siberia, starting in 1727. These waters were later named the *Bering Sea*. This sea is the northernmost part of the Pacific Ocean and the fourth largest open body of water in the world. Bering made an important discovery on his voyage. He sailed through the narrow passage between Siberia and Alaska. He could not see Alaska, which was less than 40 miles (64 km) away, because of fog. But he did prove that Asia and North America are not connected. The passage is now called the *Bering Strait*. Scientists think that ancestors of the Native Americans crossed from Asia to America, either over the frozen Strait or on a land bridge that later disappeared. At its narrowest point the Bering Strait is only 36 miles (58 km) wide.

Bering did see the volcano of St. Elias in Alaska on his second expedition in 1741. But his ship was wrecked on an island. He and many of his crew died there of scurvy. The island is now called *Bering Island*.

▶ ▶ ▶ ▶ **FIND OUT MORE** ◀ ◀ ◀ ◀
Arctic; Exploration

BERLIN

The city of Berlin is the capital of Germany. Founded in the 13th century, Berlin had become an important town in the province of Brandenburg by the 1400s. The ruling family of the province made Berlin their official home. Later it became the capital of Prussia (1701), the German Empire (1871), and after World War I, the Weimar Republic (1918). After Germany lost World War II in 1945, the city was divided, as was Germany itself. After 45 years the two Germanies reunited and Berlin once more became the capital of a united Germany in 1990.

Berlin was badly bombed during World War II and much of the city was rebuilt. In the western half, wide boulevards, tall skyscrapers, and large parks have been built. Elegant stores and theaters line the *Kurfurstendamm*, one of the city's most famous boulevards. Visitors come to see the *Tiergarten*, a park with a zoo,

a concert hall, and a public meeting hall. Nearby is the *Hansa Quarter,* a modern housing development.

The eastern half of Berlin looks drab compared to the west. Landmarks include the *Brandenburg Gate* and *Unter den Linden,* a boulevard that runs eastward from the Gate. The Brandenburg Gate used to overlook a wall that the Communists built in 1961 to separate the two halves of the city. Many East Germans died trying to escape over the wall from East to West Berlin. In 1989, the Berlin Wall was torn down and Berliners could move from one part of the city to another again.

▶ ▶ ▶ ▶ **FIND OUT MORE** ◀ ◀ ◀ ◀
Germany

BERLIN, IRVING (1888–1989)

A boy from Russia grew up and wrote the song, "God Bless America." He was Israel Baline, known to the world as Irving Berlin.

He was born in a small town in Russian Siberia. He came to America with his parents in 1893. They settled in New York City. The family was poor, so Israel and his brothers sold newspapers for pennies.

The first song published with Israel's words, or *lyrics,* earned him 37 cents. He changed his name to Irving Berlin and began writing tunes as well as words, even though he had never studied music and could barely play the piano. His song "Alexander's Ragtime Band," written in 1911, was a hit. Soon he was writing *revues* (shows with skits, songs, and dances); musical comedies, such as *Annie Get Your Gun* and *Call Me Madam,* and nearly a thousand hit songs, including "God Bless America," "Always," "White Christmas," and "Easter Parade."

▶ ▶ ▶ ▶ **FIND OUT MORE** ◀ ◀ ◀ ◀
Musical Comedy; Popular Music

◀ **Irving Berlin, the world-famous songwriter. He is seen here in a still from the World War II musical show,** *This is the Army.*

BERMUDA

Bermuda is a self-governing British dependency in the North Atlantic Ocean. It lies about 700 miles (1,130 km) southeast of New York City. There are about 300 islands in the group, but only 20 of them are inhabited. The islands form the limestone top of an underwater volcanic mountain. The largest islands—Bermuda, St. George's, St. David's, and Somerset are linked by bridges and a causeway. Hamilton, the capital, is situated on Bermuda Island.

Although low lying and hilly, Bermuda's pleasant climate and beautiful beaches attract many tourists. The average temperature stays near 70°F (20°C), which makes it a wonderful vacation spot through the year.

BERNHARDT, SARAH (1844–1923)

Her beautiful voice, the grace of her movements, and her fiery personality made Sarah Bernhardt one of the most famous actresses of her day. She was very thin, with a pale face and frizzy red hair. But she was acclaimed everywhere as "the Divine Sarah."

Her real name was Henriette-Rosine Bernard. She was born in Paris, France, and later studied acting at

▼ **The French actress, Sarah Bernhardt. Admirers called her "the Divine Sarah."**

the Paris Conservatory. After she became a star in the 1870s, she opened the Sarah Bernhardt Theater in Paris, which she managed until her death. Her most popular role was in *The Lady of the Camellias*, known in America as *Camille*.

In 1914, when Sarah Bernhardt was 70, one of her legs had to be amputated following an accident. After that, she acted from a chair but still performed all over the world. In World War I, she acted for the troops near the front line of battle and was awarded the Legion of Honor.

▶▶▶▶ **FIND OUT MORE** ◀◀◀◀
Actors and Acting; Theater

▼ The famous conductor, Leonard Bernstein

BERNSTEIN, LEONARD (1918–1990)

When Leonard Bernstein was 11, his aunt sent a piano to his house. His family was not musical, but Leonard took piano lessons, and showed such talent that music became his life. He became an internationally known pianist, conductor, and composer.

Bernstein grew up in Boston and studied music at Harvard University. In 1943, the famous conductor Bruno Walter became ill just before a concert of the New York Philharmonic Orchestra. Bernstein stepped in and conducted the orchestra without any practice and became famous overnight. After this, he performed as piano soloist with many orchestras. He also composed music. Some of his most famous works are the *Jeremiah Symphony*, the ballet *Fancy Free*, and the musical *West Side Story*.

Bernstein returned to the New York Philharmonic in 1958 as music director. He was the first American born, American trained musician to have this job. He won awards for his television series, *Young People's Concerts*. When he stopped working with the New York orchestra in

1969, he was named the *laureate* (honorary) conductor for life. His *Mass* (1971) was composed in honor of the opening of the John F. Kennedy Center for the Performing Arts in Washington, D.C.

▶▶▶▶ **FIND OUT MORE** ◀◀◀◀
Composer; Music; Musical Comedy; Orchestras and Bands

BETHUNE, MARY McLEOD (1875–1955)

Mary Bethune was a leading black educator. As a child, she worked in cotton fields owned by her parents, who had once been slaves. Mary was eager to learn, but for a long time there were no schools for black children in her hometown of Mayesville, South Carolina. Finally, a small missionary school was founded, and Mary won a scholarship there. She later won scholarships to a teachers' college in North Carolina and to the Moody Bible Institute. She married a teacher, Albertus Bethune.

Mary Bethune started her own school, in a four-room shack in Daytona Beach, Florida, in 1904. She

▼ Mary McLeod Bethune, a pioneer of black education in America.

persuaded leading townspeople to help support the school. In 1923, Mrs. Bethune's school was joined with a nearby boys' school to form the Bethune-Cookman College.

Mary Bethune was founder and president of the National Council of Negro Women and vice president of the National Association for the Advancement of Colored People (NAACP). She contributed greatly to the improvement of black education and welfare and to interracial understanding. From 1936 to 1942, she served President Franklin Roosevelt as Director of Negro Affairs.

▶▶▶▶**FIND OUT MORE**◀◀◀◀
National Association for the Advancement of Colored People

BHUTAN

Bhutan lies high in the eastern Himalaya Mountains of Asia. This tiny kingdom is about the size of Vermont and New Hampshire together. Tibet lies north of Bhutan, and India is to the south.

Bhutan is covered by ranges of snowy mountains. Some of the mountains rise more than 20,000 feet (6,000 m). Dense forests of pine and fir cover the slopes. Deer, tigers, and elephants live in the hot, wet jungles of the south. The climate ranges from bitter cold in the mountains to intense heat in the foothills and plains. The summer monsoon brings most of the yearly rainfall.

Most of the Bhutanese people are mountaineers and farmers who live in small tribal villages. They raise cattle, sheep, and yaks in the fertile valleys. The shaggy yak is important for food, clothing, and transportation. Crops must be planted in terraces because the mountainsides are so steep. Bhutan's name means "Land of the Thunder Dragon," because of its mountain storms.

Huge buildings like castles perch on the edges of high cliffs. These are monasteries called *dzongs*, where *lamas* (Buddhist priests) live. Most Bhutanese are Buddhists. They are mainly of Tibetan or Indian origin.

Bhutan is governed by a *maharajah* (ruling prince), who is helped by ministers. Bhutan's large neighbor, India, helps it deal with other countries. Bhutan was shut off from most of the world for many centuries, because it had no roads. Today, the country is linked to India by a road network and by airline service.

▶▶▶▶**FIND OUT MORE**◀◀◀◀
Asia; Buddhism; Himalaya Mountains; Tibet

BHUTAN

Capital city
Thimphu (Thimbu)
(20,000 people)

Area
18,100 square miles
(47,000 sq. km)

Population
1,442,000 people

Government
Constitutional monarchy

Natural resources
Minerals (including limestone, marble, graphite, copper, and coal), forests

Export products
Rice, fruit, timber

Unit of money
Ngultrum

Official language
Dzongkha

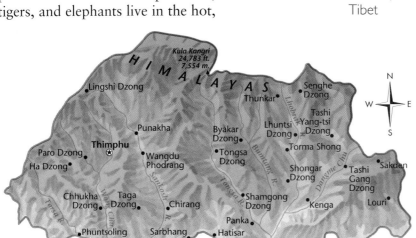

BIBLE

The Bible has been called "the greatest story ever told." It is also known as the *Scriptures*, meaning "writings." The word "bible" is the Greek word for book. The Bible really is made up of many books. These books are sacred, or holy, writings from two religions, Judaism and Christianity. Many people through the years have believed that the Bible is the word of God. There are two main parts, the Old Testament and the New Testament.

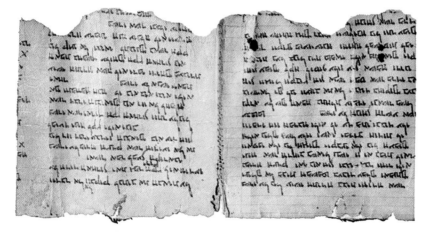

▲ Part of the Dead Sea Scrolls. These ancient writings, found in a cave beside the Dead Sea, some dating from about 200 B.C. contain the oldest-known written versions of the Old Testament.

The Authorized version of the Bible contains 774,746 words, made up of 3,566,480 letters. The word "and" occurs 46,227 times.

Books of the Bible

The *Old Testament* tells the story and the meaning of creation, and the religious history of the ancient Jews, or Hebrews. It was written on *papyrus* (material made from plants) and leather scrolls. Parts of the Old Testament may have been written down as long ago as 950 B.C. Before that, Bible stories had been told aloud for centuries. The 39 books are divided into 3 parts: the *Law*, the *Prophets*, and the *Writings*. The Jews call the five books of the Law the *Torah*. Many people believe that God gave Moses these laws, which include the Ten Commandments. The second part, the Prophets, is about the lives and acts of wise men among the Hebrews. The Writings include the Psalms and Proverbs, the Book of Job, and the Song of Songs.

The *New Testament* contains 27 books in three sections, probably all written between A.D. 50 and 100. They tell about the life of Jesus Christ, his teachings, and his followers. The first section includes the *Gospels*, accounts of the life and teachings of Christ and his followers, and the *Acts of the Apostles*. Events in the time of Christ were passed on mostly by word of mouth. The Apostles were 12 of Jesus's disciples, or followers. The first Christians wanted to be sure that Christ's teachings would not be lost, so they wrote them down. The *Epistles*, the second part, are letters to Christian communities—encouraging, teaching, and directing them. They were written by the Apostles and other followers of Christ. The third section, the *Book of Revelation*, is a *prophecy*, or vision of the future.

A third part of the Bible is called the *Apocrypha*. It is the history of the years between the times of the Old and New Testaments. These ten books might be called the fourth part of the Old Testament, but not all religions accept them as holy books. The Roman Catholic, Anglican, and Eastern Orthodox churches accept the Apocrypha. Jews accept only the 39 books of the Old Testament. Christians accept both the Old and New Testaments.

History of the Bible

The Bible has been published in almost every language. The Old Testament was translated from Hebrew into Greek before the time of Christ. This version is called the *Septuagint*, meaning "70," because 72 scholars were thought to have worked on it. Some of the Bible was written in Aramaic, an ancient, Near Eastern language. The writers of the books of Daniel and Ezra used Aramaic.

The Bible helped keep reading and writing alive even during the years after the collapse of the Western Roman Empire (about A.D. 476 to 1000). Monks living in monasteries during these centuries spent their lives copying the sacred writings. They *illuminated* (illustrated) their work with gold leaf and brightly colored letters and pictures. They filled the sides, or margins, of the pages with delicate designs.

A monk named Jerome translated the Bible from Greek into Latin about A.D. 400. This version was called the *Vulgate*, because Latin was the common (vulgar) language of much of the European world. The Vulgate was the Bible of the Catholic Church for many years. John Wycliffe translated the Bible into English for the first time in 1384. Johannes Gutenberg, the German inventor of movable type, printed a famous Bible in 1456. A copy of the *Gutenberg Bible* may be seen today in the Library of Congress. The Bible was translated into English again in 1582 and 1610. The *Douay Bible* was used by Catholics. The *King James*, or *Authorized Version*, produced by six groups of church people, was published in 1611. It is probably the most famous English Bible and is one of the great works of English literature. The first Bible printed in America, the *Algonkian Bible*, made in 1663, was a translation for Native Americans. Several new translations of the Bible have been published in this century. Among these are the *Revised Standard Version* in 1952 and 1973, the *New English Bible* in 1961 and 1970, *The New American Bible* in 1970, and the *New Revised Standard Version* in 1990. These are written in modern English.

The *Dead Sea Scrolls,* texts written on papyrus and vellum, as long ago as 200 years before Christ, were discovered in 1947. They include fragments of nearly all the books of the Old Testament. They have helped scholars make more accurate translations of the Old Testament.

More copies of the Bible in all its forms have been sold than any other book ever written. The books of the Bible were written by many people, in many different kinds of writing— essays, stories, poetry, history, drama, laws, songs, and prophecies. Daniel in the lion's den, Jonah and the Whale, and David and Goliath are inspiring stories of faith. The Bible has been a guide, and an inspiration, for many of the different peoples of the world.

►►►► **FIND OUT MORE** ◄◄◄◄
Apostles; Christianity; Dead Sea Scrolls; Jesus Christ; Jewish History; Judaism

BIBLIOGRAPHY

At the end of a nonfiction book, there is often a list of other books. This list is a *bibliography*. It tells you that the author of the book studied the books on the list to learn more about the subject. Also, the list can help the reader to find out more about the subject. You will find bibliography boxes with some of the articles in this encyclopedia.

Each book, pamphlet, or magazine article has a separate *entry*, or item, on the bibliography list. Every entry has the same plan. First, it tells who wrote the book, pamphlet, or article, and what the title is. It then tells the city where the book was published, the name of the publishing company, and the date of publication. Here is a sample entry for a bibliography:

White, E.B. *Charlotte's Web.* New York: Harper Bros., 1952.

►►►► **FIND OUT MORE** ◄◄◄◄
Book; Catalog; Library

◄ A page from the *Book of Kells*, an illuminated copy of the Gospels made by monks in Ireland over 1,000 years ago. It shows St. John the Evangelist surrounded by beautiful designs.

▲ Some Old Testament Bible stories are also found in the stories of other ancient religions. The Sumerians told the story of The Great Flood. Noah is called Utnapishtim in the Sumerian story. He is warned by the gods to build a boat (the ark in the story of Noah) to escape the flood. After the flood, a bird finds dry land, and they are saved.

A dandyhorse

BICYCLE

People in the United States ride bicycles mostly for fun. But people in many other countries ride bicycles to get where they have to go—to work, to school, or to the market. In some parts of Europe, Asia, and South America people depend more on bicycles than on automobiles. Today's bicycle is a quick, safe way to get from place to place, but this was not always so.

The first bicycle was built in Europe about 1690. The rider sat on a wooden seat and pushed the bicycle along with his feet. This "walking machine" had no brakes, no pedals, and no handlebar. One hundred years later, inventors started working again. An Englishman contributed a gear chain connecting the wheels. A Scotsman attached pedals to the rear wheel of a bicycle, and for the first time a rider did not have to touch the ground. A Frenchman moved the pedals to the front wheel, but the wheels were made of iron and people called his bicycle the *boneshaker*, because it was so uncomfortable and bumpy to ride.

A penny-farthing

▲ The dandyhorse or *draisine* of 1817 looked like a bicycle but had no pedals. The Matchless ordinary or *penny-farthing* of 1883 had a huge front wheel and solid tires.

▼ An advertisement of 1890 for J. K. Starley's new bicycle. For the first time, bicycles had wheels of equal size.

▲ A closeup of the back wheel of a road bicycle, showing the gears. Gears make it easier for the rider to pedal at different speeds.

Bicycles were becoming popular. They still, however, did not look like bicycles of today. The front wheel was about 6 feet (2m) high, and the rear wheel was quite small. Then, in 1885, J.K. Starley of Great Britain made a bicycle with both wheels about the same size. With the addition of air-filled rubber tires and a chain-driven gear, bicycles became much safer and more comfortable vehicles, and were soon being ridden by many people.

Bicycle racing became a recognized sport in the 1890s. Today, races are held on indoor and outdoor tracks, with steeply banked curves and short straightaways. Even more exciting are the major road races, held mainly in Europe. The best racers compete in the *Tour de France* each year, traveling more than 3,000 miles (4,800 km) in about three weeks. A U.S. rider, Greg LeMond, has won the Tour de France three times, the first American to win the race.

The sport of racing has produced bicycles that have made riding easier. Very light, aluminum, 14- or 16-speed bicycles are common. They originally were used only by serious racers. Today, sturdier, more rugged bicycles, such as *mountain bikes,* are very popular.

For most people, bicycling is just fun in the open air. Bicycling is a good way to tour the U.S. and other countries. Bicycle tourists either camp out overnight or stay at inexpensive lodgings called *youth hostels.* Today, people are aware that bicycles are a good means of transportation. Bicycling helps keep you fit and does not add to air pollution or noise problems.

Saddle

Seat post

Brakes

Frame

Cogs

Pedals

Handlebars

Gear levers

Brake levers

Shock absorber

Chain rings

Chain

Gears

Rim

Spoke

▲ Today's mountain bike has a light aluminum frame, shock absorbers (for traveling over rough terrain) and up to 21 gears.

▼ Cyclists from all over the world take part in the *Tour de France* road race, a test of endurance for both rider and machine.

QUIZ

1. The word bicycle means "two-wheeled." What do we call a one-wheeled vehicle? And one with three wheels?
2. When and where was the first bicycle built?
3. When is the Tour de France held?
4. Modern bikes have brake levers on the handlebars, with brake cables leading to the back wheel. On simpler bikes, how do you brake?

(Answers on page 384)

▲ Chimes ring out from Big Ben, one of the world's most famous clocks. Its bell is heard hourly around the British Houses of Parliament in London and is carried around the world on BBC overseas radio broadcasts.

▼ Snooker, like pool, is derived from billiards. It is played on a special table and the object is to knock colored balls into pockets using a cue and cue ball.

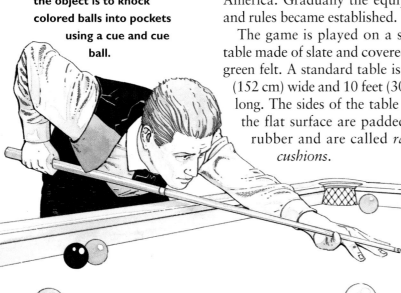

BIG BEN

One of the most famous sights in London, England, is a clock tower attached to the Houses of Parliament. In it is a huge bell called *Big Ben*. It weighs 13$\frac{1}{2}$ tons (12.2 metric tons). Members of Parliament named it after Sir Benjamin Hall, a large man who was Commissioner of Public Works when the bell was installed in 1859.

The name *Big Ben* is now used also for the giant clock on the Parliament tower. The hour hands are 9 feet (2.7 m) long, and the minute hands are 14 feet (4.3 m) long. Lord Grimthorpe, a lawyer, designed it. The Big Ben clock is usually very accurate. But once it did lose five minutes—when a flock of starlings settled on one of its hands.

BILLIARD GAMES

Billiards is a game for two or four players. It requires good coordination and many hours of practice. Some historians believe billiards was developed in England more than 600 years ago, in an attempt to make lawn bowling an indoor game. Early colonists from England, France, and Spain brought the game with them to America. Gradually the equipment and rules became established.

The game is played on a special table made of slate and covered with green felt. A standard table is 5 feet (152 cm) wide and 10 feet (305 cm) long. The sides of the table above the flat surface are padded with rubber and are called *rails* or *cushions*.

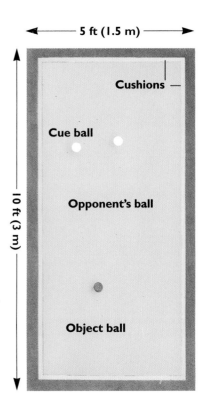

▲ The dimensions of a billiard table. All tables are twice as long as they are wide.

There are three billiard balls. One is red. The other two are white. One of the white ones has two red dots on it. A player uses a *cue* (a long wooden stick) to hit the cue ball, one of the white ones. He makes a point if his cue ball touches the other two balls before it stops rolling. A game is usually 50 or 100 points.

A popular variation of billiards is *pocket billiards,* or *pool.* The players use the same kind of cue sticks. The table is similar, but it is smaller and has six pockets, one in each corner and one halfway down each long side.

Pool players use 15 numbered balls and one cue ball. The cue ball is white, and the numbered balls are different colors. Balls 1 through 8 are solid colors, each with its number showing. Balls 9 through 15 are white with colored stripes, and the numbers are on the stripes. The object in most pool games is to hit the cue ball into the other balls and knock them into the pockets, without the cue ball's dropping in.

The game known as *snooker* is

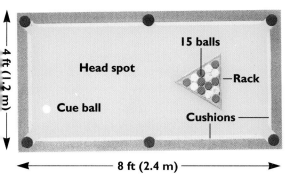

Head spot

15 balls

Rack

Cue ball

Cushions

4 ft (1.2 m)

8 ft (2.4 m)

popular in Britain, Canada, and Australia. Snooker is played with 22 balls: one white (which is the cue ball), 15 red, and 6 colors. The colors are valued by the points they score when knocked into a pocket. A red ball scores 1, yellow 2, green 3, brown 4, blue 5, pink 6, and black 7. Each player tries first to knock a red ball into a pocket, followed by one of the colors, followed by another red, and so on. Each red pocketed stays off the table, but colors are put back until all reds have been removed.

▶▶▶▶ **FIND OUT MORE** ◀◀◀◀
Games

BILL OF RIGHTS

The first ten Amendments to the Constitution of the United States are also called the *Bill of Rights*. Most of these rights protect the individual citizen against the government. Laws passed by Congress in conflict with the Bill of Rights may be *overruled* (declared unconstitutional) by the United States Supreme Court.

The rights guaranteed in the first ten Amendments are rights that the English had earned over many centuries, beginning with the Magna Carta in 1215. Some of the rights had been written into the charters of the various colonies. When the U.S. Constitution was completed in 1789, many people wanted the rights included so that the Federal Government would not become too power-

ful. The Constitution was accepted by the states with the understanding that Amendments, stating the rights of the people, would be made promptly. The ten Amendments making up the Bill of Rights were added in 1791.

The first Amendment forbids the government to interfere with freedom of speech, freedom of the press, and freedom of religion. The Amendment also guarantees the right to ask the government for justice and to demonstrate peaceably. The second Amendment says that citizens have a right to possess arms (weapons). The third Amendment says that citizens cannot be forced to provide room and board for soldiers in their homes. The fourth guarantees that people or their property cannot be searched or taken away without a *warrant* (permission) that has been issued by a law officer.

The fifth, sixth, seventh, and eighth Amendments have to do with fair and just treatment in the courts of law. A person cannot be tried twice for the same crime and cannot be forced to *testify* (speak out) against himself. He or she must be tried by a jury if desired, and the trial must be held in the area where the crime was committed unless a judge allows a change of venue. Finally, he or she must not be subjected to cruel and unusual punishment.

The ninth Amendment says that any rights not specifically mentioned in the Bill of Rights or the Constitution belong to the people. The tenth Amendment provides that powers not given specifically to the federal government shall belong to the States and the people.

▶▶▶▶ **FIND OUT MORE** ◀◀◀◀
Civil Rights; Constitution, United States; Court System; Four Freedoms; States' Rights

◀ **A pool table is smaller than a billiard table. The 15 numbered balls are arranged in a triangle at the start of the game. The first player must shoot the cue ball into the triangle of balls. This shot is called a "break."**

◀ **The 15 numbered balls used in pool. The balls were once made of ivory but are now manufactured from a plastic material. They weigh between 5½ and 6 ounces (160 to 170 g).**

The first ten amendments to the United States Constitution became the law of the land on December 15, 1791. The amendments were known as the Bill of Rights, a summary of the basic rights held by all United States citizens. There were originally 12 amendments, but two that changed the method of electing members of Congress were rejected.

▲ The word *binary* comes from the Latin word *bini*, meaning "two at a time." The binary system uses only two numerals, 0 and 1. With a binary number, the digit on the right has the value one, the next number going left is two times larger, and so on. Therefore, when you move a numeral one place to the left you multiply its value by two.

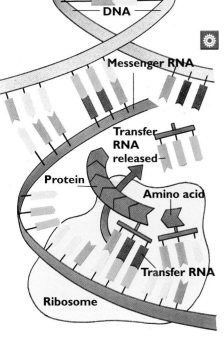

DNA

Messenger RNA

Transfer RNA released

Protein

Amino acid

Transfer RNA

Ribosome

◄ DNA and RNA control heredity and life itself. DNA provides the "plan" from which a new organism is made. RNA carries instructions from genes on the strand of DNA. We all have slightly different genes, so we all look different.

BINARY SYSTEM

The word *decimal* describes the system based on powers of ten that we use for writing down numbers. In the decimal system, the value of each number changes according to its position in the figure as a whole. For example, the numerals 2 and 6 can give the figure 26. If we turn them around we get 62. The numerals are the same but their position makes all the difference. You multiply a number by 10 by moving it one place to the left. The numeral 1 by itself is just 1. Move it one place to the left and it becomes 10 times 1, or 10. Move it another place to the left and it becomes 100, and so on.

In the binary system, when you move a numeral one place to the left you multiply its value by two. A 1 by itself is 1. Move it one place to the left and it becomes 1 times 2, or 2. It is written 10. Move it another place to the left and it becomes 1 times 2 times 2, or 4. This is written 100. Any number can be written in binary. The number 18 is 10010.

▶▶▶▶ **FIND OUT MORE** ◄◄◄◄
Arithmetic; Computer; Decimal Number

BIOCHEMISTRY

All living things are made of tiny blocks of matter called *cells*. The activities that mean "this object is alive" take place in the cells. The activities are mainly chemical changes, and they occur in different ways in different living things. Biochemistry is the study of the chemical reactions and biological processes that occur in the cells of all living things.

Biochemists seek to know how living things grow, and how their chemical structures keep them alive. They have traced the way we digest food and how the food is chemically burned to release energy. They have followed oxygen from the air to the cell, where it is used to burn food. They have discovered substances called *enzymes* and *hormones*, which direct how the cell will use the energy. From this work, scientists have been able to learn what kinds of food make people healthy. They

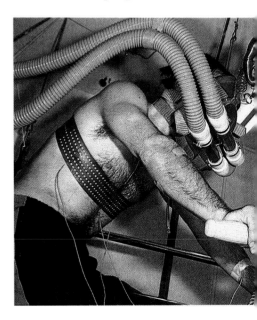

▲ An experiment to look at the chemical changes that take place during respiration or breathing.

have learned the value of calories, vitamins, and minerals. They have developed medicines that help cells do their work properly.

Biochemists study special molecules in the cell, called *nucleic acids*. The nucleic acids are very complex, and scientists have found that they control all growth and reproduction. One form of nucleic acid—RNA (ribonucleic acid) is found throughout the cell; it controls protein-making. DNA (deoxyribonucleic acid), another form of nucleic acid, is found only in the nucleus. It carries and passes a kind of "blueprint" of the plan of a living thing from one generation to the next in the form of *genes*. It is the substance that makes you a human being who is different from any other human being.

Biochemistry is one of the most exciting sciences today. New questions are popping up in biochemists' laboratories everywhere. What can prevent birth defects? How does the diet of a poorly fed child affect intelligence? Answers to these and a thousand other questions are being pieced together one step at a time by biochemists.

▶▶▶▶ **FIND OUT MORE** ◀◀◀◀
Cell; Digestion; Enzyme; Genetics; Growth; Hormone; Life; Respiration

BIOGRAPHY

A *biography* is a life history of one person written by another. An *autobiography* (*auto* means "self") is a life history written by the person the story is about. A biography should include *what* happened, and *where* and *when* these events took place, but should read like an adventure story.

In the past, biographies were often written to teach a lesson. These were called *didactic* biographies. Sometimes, the facts in these books were exaggerated. For example, the famous biography of George Washington, written about 1800 by Parson Weems, told the story about George chopping down his father's cherry tree. This old tale was not true. Another fault of some older biographies was their "perfect image." Authors left out important facts about a person if they were not flattering.

A good biography of today tells as many facts, good and bad, as possible.

▶▶▶▶ **FIND OUT MORE** ◀◀◀◀
Diary; Legend; Literature

LEARN BY DOING

Interview a relative or friend, and then try to write a short biography about him or her. Remember, you, as the author, have two jobs: to give the facts and to make them interesting to your readers.

⚙ BIOLOGY

More than a million different kinds of animals and more than 330,000 different kinds of plants live on Earth. The science that studies all these living organisms and their relationship to each other is called *biology*. It is the science of life.

Biologists place every known organism into one of three large groups, called *kingdoms*. The two largest of these kingdoms are the *Plant Kingdom*, containing all plants, and the *Animal Kingdom*, containing all animals. Some organisms, so tiny they can only be seen with a microscope, do not act exactly like plants or animals. Biologists group these particular living things into the *Protist Kingdom*. *Zoology* is the study of the members of the Animal Kingdom. *Botany* is the study of the Plant Kingdom. *Taxonomists* are biologists whose special work is to group all living things into their proper kingdoms and subgroups.

Some biologists do not study just zoology or botany—they study both plants and animals. Every living thing is made up of cells. *Cytology* is the study of cells, what they look like, and how they function or work. Cells fit together in structures that give daisies, pigeons, people, and all other living things their special shapes. The study of the structure of living things is *anatomy*. All living things have functions such as digestion, growth, respiration, and reproduction. *Biochemistry* and *physiology* are studies of these functions. Diseases can cause living things to stop functioning or to function inefficiently. *Pathology* is the study of how

Bat wing

Bird wing

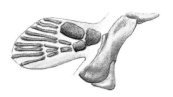

Lobe-finned fish

Insect wing

▲ Animals that fly or swim need broad, wide surfaces that give a strong push against air or water. They have, therefore, developed wings or fins and tails for this purpose. Although the wings of the fliers or the fins of the swimmers differ in structure, they serve similar functions.

SOME BIOLOGICAL SCIENCES

Evolution
Study of the process of change in living creatures

Biosociology
Study of the environments of groups of living things

Paleontology
Study of fossils

Parasitology
Study of parasites

Anatomy
Study of the structures of plants and animals

Bacteriology
Study of bacteria

Embryology
Study of the formation and development of living things before birth

Genetics
Study of heredity

Ecology
Study of the relationships between living things and their environments

Cytology
Study of cells

▼ **Biology helps us understand how living things relate to one another and their environment. This diagram shows how energy is passed along**

Energy source

Carnivores (meat-eaters)

Herbivores (plant-eaters)

Producers (plants)

Detritivores (living things that eat decayed animals and plants).

▲ **Plants turn sunlight into energy. This energy is passed on to plant-eating animals who in turn, pass it on to meat-eating animals. When animals and plants die, they are broken down by detritivores, and their nutrients are released into the soil.**

diseases affect living things and what can be done to prevent and cure disease.

Why do some people have blue eyes and others brown ones? Why is every person, cow, and oak tree different from every other person, cow, and oak tree? *Genetics* is the study of these differences. How can so many different kinds of living things exist in the world at once? In how many different ways do all these organisms depend upon one another for survival? These questions and many others are answered by *ecology*.

Other biologists study theories of *evolution*, the idea that change affects living things over millions of years. About 60 million years ago the ancestors of horses were only as big as dogs. For what reason have these animals grown larger? The study of evolution tries to answer such questions.

▶▶▶▶ **FIND OUT MORE** ◀◀◀◀
Bacteria; Biochemistry; Botany; Cell; Ecology; Evolution; Fossil; Genetics; Life; Parasite; Protist; Zoology

BIOLUMINESCENCE

Many types of living organisms have the ability to glow in the dark, or *luminesce*. The process producing this light is called *bioluminescence*. It produces a cold light of various colors by means of chemical reactions inside the organism. Light is produced when *enzymes* break down a substance called *luciferin*. Bioluminescence is responsible for the flashing tail lights of the firefly, which is used to attract a mate, and for the brilliant lights of many deep-sea fishes. These lights help the fish to find other fish in total darkness and to find food. Light is produced in special organs, arranged so that the pattern of light is easily recognized by other creatures.

Some types of marine *plankton*, or tiny floating animals and plants, luminesce brightly when the water is disturbed by a swimmer or a boat. Many *bacteria* and *fungi* also produce light by bioluminescence. The same chemical process has been copied by chemists to produce cold lights that are used for emergency lighting. These lights glow brightly until all the light-producing chemicals in them are used up.

▶▶▶▶ **FIND OUT MORE** ◀◀◀◀
Deep-Sea Life

▲ **Many deep-sea fish carry lights. This fish produces a beam of red light that it uses to find food in the sunless waters of the deep sea.**

BIRD

The world has about 9,000 kinds of the feathered creatures called birds. About 800 *species* (kinds) live in North America alone. One of these is the tiny hummingbird, which weighs not much more than three sheets of typewriter paper. North America's tallest bird is the whooping crane. It stands about 5 feet (1.5 m), and has a wingspan of 90 inches (2.3 m). It is one of the rarest birds in the world.

The many different kinds of birds in the world all belong to a class in the animal kingdom known as *Aves* (Latin for birds). This class is then divided into smaller groups, known as *orders*. Most *ornithologists* (scientists who study birds) recognize about 28 orders of living birds.

Many ornithologists start the grouping of birds with the orders that are *extinct,* or gone, and are found only as fossils. The next orders of birds are those that do not fly but can walk, run, or swim. Some of these, such as penguins, can walk and swim. The flying bird orders complete the classification. Of the flightless birds, the best known examples include the ostrich, emu, kiwi, and rhea. The moa of New Zealand belonged to this group but is now extinct. A penguin does not fly but instead uses its wings to help it swim underwater.

Most birds can fly. It is the marvel of flight that makes them unusual among the warm-blooded animals. Have you wondered why birds, almost alone among the warm-blooded animals, can fly? It is because birds have feathers; wings; a breastbone with a special ridge of bone called the *keel;* strong muscles; hollow, but strong, bones; a brain largely used for seeing, hearing, and motion control; and even specialized breathing organs. The bird's whole body is designed for flight. All these special body organs must be present and work together for a bird to fly. The birds we know today probably developed from ancient reptiles many millions of years ago. The oldest known birdlike creature, called *Archaeopteryx,* had a skeleton like a reptile, with a backbone that extended into a tail. Birds still have scaly feet like reptiles.

▼ **The downstroke of a bird's wing forces air down and back, causing the bird to be pushed up and forward. The upstroke is less powerful, so the air slips past and does not push the bird down again.**

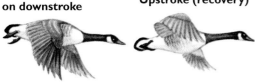

Feathers together on downstroke

Upstroke (recovery)

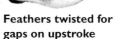

Feathers twisted for gaps on upstroke

Downstroke (lift)

▲ The kiwi lives only in New Zealand. It has no tail and it cannot fly. It sleeps by day and feeds at night.

▲ Penguins are flightless seabirds. Their wings have evolved into powerful flippers that propel them through water at great speeds.

▲ In shallow lakes, flamingos construct mud nest mounds with a saucer-shaped pit in the top for the eggs.

▶ The secretary bird lives on the open savanna of Africa and eats locusts, lizards, snakes and rats.

Flight is thought to have developed in this way: First, birds ran swiftly. Next, they were able to make long, wing-flapping leaps. Perhaps some leaps were "glides" from a high tree to one not so high. Finally, birds were able to fly. True flight took a long, long time to develop.

Where Birds Are Found

Birds are able to live in most parts of the world. Penguins live in Antarctica, the icy region around the South Pole. The equator is home to many species of brilliantly colored tropical birds. A species of quail is found in the desert. The albatross, a true sea bird, stays on or above its watery habitat for months at a time, without ever coming to land. The water ouzel or dipper, found in the American West, lives near a stream. It actually runs along a streambed at times, looking for food.

Some birds are found in different places at different times of the year. Both the tiny hummingbird and the huge whooping crane *migrate* (make long flights) twice a year. They fly north each spring to mate and raise their young. In the fall, they fly south to pass the winter. Some birds fly thousands of miles between their winter and summer homes. The golden plover nests far north in the Arctic tundra. It winters in southern South America, more than 7,000 miles (11,000 km) away. At the same time, its *plumage* (feathers) changes from dark colors to lighter colors. Many birds migrate to find the same kind of environment for winter and summer.

Ways of Life

Every bird has its place in nature. It has its very own *ecological niche* (place in the plant and animal community). Some birds are *predatory*, meaning they kill other animals for food. The golden eagle is a predator; it kills rabbits and rodents. Hawks and owls prey on rats, mice, and some insects. Predators help to reduce the number of rodents and control the damage done by rodents to crops and stored foods. Diving ducks plunge to depths of 30 feet (9 m) for the plants they eat. Thrushes are the greatest eaters of insects. Bluejays and cardinals are seed-eaters. Geese eat grass and seeds. And hummingbirds drain nectar from flowers. The feet and beaks of birds vary with the way the animals live.

Many birds receive their common names because of their habits. The turnstone, for example, is a shorebird that turns over pebbles as it walks along the beach. The bobwhite, or common quail gets its name from its call. The honeyguide of Africa leads both people and badgers to trees in which there is wild honey. The

burrowing owl often makes use of the burrows made by prairie dogs.

Nests and Eggs

Some birds have little or no need for nests. Others build elaborate ones. The nest of some penguins is nothing more than a bare rock. A depression in the ground, lined with wild grasses, seems to satisfy the wild turkey. The mound-building birds of Australia scrape together piles of leaves and twigs. The small bushtit hangs grass pockets on branches. And the cowbird does not bother with any form of nest. The

▲ Weaver birds are small, sparrowlike birds that live in Africa and Asia. They are named after the basket-shaped nests that the male "weaves" from strands of grass or palm fronds.

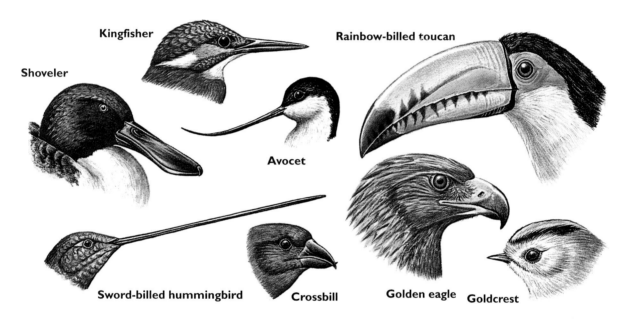

Shoveler
Kingfisher
Rainbow-billed toucan
Avocet
Sword-billed hummingbird
Crossbill
Golden eagle
Goldcrest

female lays her eggs in the nest of another species when the rightful owner is away. Some orioles build large community "apartment-house" nests.

The number of eggs a female bird lays depends upon the species. Petrels lay only a single egg. It is usually white and is deposited in a nest, for example, made of grass and twigs. Sometimes the egg of the storm petrel is lightly marked with purple. European widgeons lay seven or eight buff-colored eggs. American widgeons, or baldpates, may lay as many as 18 eggs, although the average is 10. Many birds, such as the common robin, lay three, four, or five eggs.

Hazards of Bird Life

Young birds face dangers. They may be prey for snakes, mammals, or even other birds. The nest of a perching bird may be a long way from the ground, and it is easy to fall out of. One of the great dangers to waterfowl is a long, dry, hot spell. The drainage of marshes ruins the habitat of marsh dwellers such as bitterns, marsh wrens, and red-winged blackbirds.

Adult birds, too, face dangers. Strong light confuses night-flying birds, causing them to crash against obstacles. Birds that migrate at night, including many favorite songbirds, are sometimes killed flying into tele-

▲ Birds' beaks have many different shapes and are well suited to their feeding habits. The hummingbird, for example, has a long, narrow beak that it uses to probe for nectar. The crossbill cracks seeds with its strong crooked bill, and the golden eagle tears flesh with its powerful hooked beak.

▲ **Oil spills are a serious threat to wildlife, harming and killing many species of birds.**

▲ **A tiny ruby-throated hummingbird.**

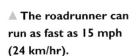

▲ **The roadrunner can run as fast as 15 mph (24 km/hr).**

▼ **A brown pelican. It uses the pouch beneath its bill as a net to catch fish.**

vision towers and other tall structures, or even airplanes. Heavy storms, diseases, and predatory animals are also bird killers. And today, pollution, such as oil spills at sea, is responsible for many bird deaths.

Many birds in North America are protected because lands have been set aside for them. These lands, called National Wildlife Refuges, provide life's essentials for many birds. Some states have laws protecting songbirds. All states regulate the hunting seasons on nonmigratory birds. The federal government administers the laws protecting migratory birds. And treaties with Canada and Mexico protect more than 50 different species. Even so, there are many birds that are in danger of becoming extinct. The huge California condor has become so rare that efforts are being made to rear chicks in captivity to save the species from dying out. The Everglades kite, rare already, came even closer to extinction in 1971, when its Florida home went through a long, dry period. Even the national bird of the United States, the bald eagle, is becoming more scarce. The bald eagles, with white feather caps on their heads, have been shot illegally and poisoned by harmful chemicals used by farmers. So now people are doing their best to protect the eagles.

▶ ▶ ▶ ▶ **FIND OUT MORE** ◀ ◀ ◀ ◀
Ecology see Animal Homes; City Wildlife; Ecology; Migration; Wilderness Area
Land Birds see Birds of Prey; Flightless Birds; Game Birds; Garden Birds; Hummingbird; Owl; Parrots and Parakeets; Pigeon; Poultry; Stork
Water Birds see Crane; Ducks and Geese; Gulls and Terns; Pelican; Penguin; Seabirds; Water Birds
Zoology see Animal Defenses; Animal Kingdom; Animal Voices; Egg; Evolution; Feather; Hands and Feet; Skeleton

BIRD WATCHING

SEE NATURE STUDY

BIRDS OF PREY

Some birds feed on small animals and other birds. They are called *birds of prey*. They help to control the number of small birds and animals. These birds form one large *order* (group) of birds. Several kinds of birds are included. All of them are flesh-eaters with sharply hooked, curved bills, and strong, sharp, curved claws. Most of them eat only meat, but some eat vegetables, too. Owls are not included in the same order, but they are also flesh-eating hunters.

Wing shapes tell how birds of prey hunt. Birds with long, narrow wings fly fast. They capture their prey in the air. Those with short, rounded wings can turn sharply. They attack close to the ground where they can corner their prey. Birds with broad wings soar high above the ground. These birds usually feed on *carrion*, or dead animals.

Eagles and Falcons

Bald eagles and *golden eagles* are the only eagles found in North America. They are America's largest birds, except for the California condor. The bald eagle is not really bald—its head and neck are covered with pure white feathers. Bald eagles live in the mild-climate areas of North America. Males weigh up to 8 pounds (3.6 kg) and have a wingspan of 7 feet (2.1 m). Females are larger, up to 12 pounds (5.4 kg). The bald eagle is the national bird of the United States, but it is very rare because many of these birds have been shot by hunters. Also, a high concentration of DDT (a chemical used to kill insect pests) found in eagles has made them lay thin-shelled eggs that do not hatch. The golden eagle lives in the mountains in Europe, Asia, and Africa, as well as North America. The adult is dark brown with golden tints. Eagles' nests are called *aeries*. Bald eagles usually build their aeries in tall trees, near water. Golden eagles prefer rock ledges.

Falcons look like streamlined hawks. They flap their wings more quickly than hawks. Their wings are also longer and more pointed than hawks' wings and their tails are longer. *Gyrfalcons* are the largest falcons. They live in the Arctic and eat rodents and smaller birds. *Sparrow*

hawks are small North American falcons. They perch on telephone poles and trees, then race off after flying insects they spot with their sharp eyes. The *duck hawk*, or *peregrine falcon*, swoops down on its favorite prey of ducks, geese, and other birds at 225 miles an hour (362 km/hr)!

Hunters and Fishers

The *secretary bird* of Africa is the only member of its family, which means that no other birds are classified with it. The secretary bird, with gray and black plumage, has a long neck and long legs. It is about 4 feet (1.2 m) tall. It is the only bird of prey that hunts on foot. Secretary birds kill harmful insects and snakes.

One bird-of-prey family includes all kites, hawks, eagles, and Old World vultures. Kites are found all over the world. Four kinds live in

> Most birds of prey have very sharp eyesight. It has been said that a hawk's vision can be likened to that of a man using binoculars that show things eight times their size.

◁ The bald eagle can be found only in North America. Many bald eagles have been killed by hunters and trappers. It is now a very rare species, and is protected by federal laws.

◁ The gyrfalcon is the largest of the falcons found in northern Europe, Scandinavia, Siberia, and northern Canada. It hunts ptarmigan, lemmings, rabbits, and sea birds and normally nests on rock ledges.

Bald eagle

Turkey vulture

Prairie Falcon

▲ Although the hooked beaks of the birds of prey look extremely dangerous, the birds depend on their talons as their main weapon.

▼ The California condor breeds once every other year and lays only one egg. Because the species is dying out, it is protected by law.

North America. Kites have long, narrow wings. Kites hunt in the air. *Mississippi* and *white-tailed kites* look much like falcons. Black and purple *swallow-tailed kites* have forked tails. The broad-winged *Everglades kites* are almost extinct. Kites do not dive headfirst at their prey. They swoop downward, feet first, and grab with their powerful claws.

Male hawks are usually smaller than females. Males range from 10 to 22 inches (25 to 56 cm) long. Their wings are broader than a falcon's and a little bit rounder. Hawks are strong fliers and have excellent eyesight. Hawks eat all of their prey, including the bones and fur or feathers. They vomit balls, or *pellets*, of the portions they cannot digest.

North American hawks are divided into two large groups, bird hawks and buzzard hawks. *Buzzard hawks* have large bodies, broad, rounded wings, and broad tails. The *red-tailed, red-shouldered, white-tailed,* and *black* hawks are all buzzard hawks. Buzzard hawks soar overhead and dive at their prey. *Bird hawks* have long tails and short wings. They glide frequently. The *goshawk* is the largest of the bird hawks. *Sharp-shinned hawks* often prey on pigeons, birds as big as the hawks themselves. The *harrier hawks*, found in many parts of the world, have long, pointed wings. The only North American harrier is the *marsh hawk*, which swoops low over the ground as it hunts. *Ospreys*, or

▲ The golden eagle lives in open mountainous country and hunts over a wide area.

fish hawks, are found near water all over the world. They eat only fish and are expert fishers. Ospreys fly high over the water, then dive on their prey, sometimes diving completely underwater to catch a meal.

Carrion Eaters

Vultures, or *buzzards*, live in most warm parts of the world. They eat carrion. They can see dead animals as they soar very high in the sky. Their heads are bald. Vultures build no nests but hatch their young on the ground, on rock, or in caves.

The *California condor* is the largest North American land bird. It can be more than 50 inches (1.25 m) long, and has a wingspan of 8 to 11 feet (2.4 to 3.3 m). These condors sometimes live 50 years. Females lay one egg, which both

◄ The earliest bird discovered so far is the *Archaeopteryx*, which means "ancient feather." It was a very primitive bird. Scientists believe it may have looked like this reconstruction, and that it is the missing link between reptiles and birds.

parents incubate. California condors are almost extinct. *Turkey vultures*, however, are very common and live almost everywhere in the U.S. They are about 30 inches (76 cm) long. They have black feathers and red heads. *Black vultures* live in the southern U.S. and Central and South America. They sometimes live in cities, where they feed on garbage. Old World vultures, such as the Egyptian vulture and the lammergeier, are also carrion eaters, but they are members of the *hawk* family.

▶ ▶ ▶ ▶ **FIND OUT MORE** ◄ ◄ ◄ ◄
Bird; Birds of the Past; Falconry; Owl

BIRDS OF THE PAST

The beautiful red cardinal singing in the maple tree does not look like the black garter snake crawling on the ground. But birds and reptiles are related. Both hatch from eggs. Both have skin without sweat glands. They have similar bone structures and digestive systems. But important changes occurred, which separated birds from reptiles.

The first evidence of birdlike creatures is thought to be about 150 million years ago. A *fossil* (the remains of an animal or plant) called *Archaeopteryx* was discovered in

Germany in the nineteenth century. This ancient animal had a tail like that of a lizard, a jaw with teeth, and feathers. It was about the size of a crow and could probably glide through the air, traveling from a high tree to a lower one. Its forelegs were more like hands than wings, and claws stuck out from the "wing" edge.

Fossils of birdlike creatures from the next 30 or 40 million years are missing. Birds' bones are not often fossilized because they are easily smashed. Then, fossils found of two North American creatures, showed what was happening to birds. *Hesperornis regalis* probably lived 60 to 120 million years ago. It was about 6 feet (1.8 m) tall. It could not fly, but it could swim. It had the beginnings of a beak. *Ichthyornis victor* was a flying bird that looked like a gull.

By 60 million years ago, birds were much like those of today. Light hollow beaks had replaced jaws with teeth by that time. The lizardlike tail had shortened. The claws had disappeared from the wings. The part of the brain that controls vision and flying had increased in size. Birds had become fast, skillful flyers because they had developed ridges on their

▼ The moa was found in New Zealand, where it was hunted by Maoris for food until it became extinct. Moas could grow up to 10 feet (3m) tall. They could not fly because they had tiny wings, but they had long, thick legs and could run very fast.

▲ The dodo was discovered about 400 years ago. It was as big as a turkey, and could not fly because it did not have true wings. Dodos were killed for food, and by the 1690s were extinct.

▼ A Chinese government poster, part of an advertising campaign to promote birth control by encouraging couples to have only one child. For several years, it has been illegal for Chinese people to have more children. Other governments tried to restrict population growth but only some have been successful.

breastbones, to which strong muscles could be attached.

After birds learned to fly, some of them lost the power and adapted to a ground or water existence. Other birds evolved into the great variety of birds living today. In the past 200 years, human destruction has caused many birds to become extinct.

Passenger pigeons by the millions lived in the eastern half of the United States 100 years ago. They fed on acorns and beechtree nuts. People cut down the beech trees and the oaks, and killed millions of these birds for food. The last passenger pigeon, who was named Martha, died in a zoo in 1914.

The dodo, a flightless bird of Mauritius Island in the Indian Ocean, was killed off in the 1600s. The Carolina parakeet was once numerous in the South, but it is extinct now because people wanted its colorful feathers. The great auk and Labrador duck are some other extinct birds, killed off by people. The Eskimo curlew may be extinct now, and over 50 other American species are in danger of soon becoming extinct.

▶▶▶▶ **FIND OUT MORE** ◀◀◀◀
Bird; Evolution; Fossil; Flightless Birds; Reptile

BIRTH CONTROL

A couple decide that they are not yet able to bring up a child until they move from their small apartment. Government officials in a poor country see starving children and no food to give them. A woman is told by her doctor that becoming pregnant might harm her health.

These people might decide that the answer to their problem is to prevent the birth of children. This type of prevention, or regulation, is called *birth control. Family planning* and *planned parenthood* are two other names for birth control. Many American couples practice some form of birth control.

A woman becomes pregnant when an egg produced by one of her two *ovaries* is fertilized by one of the millions of sperm released by a man during sexual intercourse. That moment when the egg is fertilized is called *conception.* The fertilized egg travels down to the woman's *uterus,* or womb. There it will grow and develop into a baby who will be born about nine months later. During that time the child developing in the womb is called a *fetus.*

There are many types of birth control. One of the most widely used are *contraceptives.* The word contraceptives means "against conception." Contraceptives prevent a man's sperm from fertilizing a woman's egg.

Oral contraceptives, or *birth control pills,* work by using hormones to change the behavior of the egg. A *condom,* on the other hand, affects the sperm. It is a thin sheath of rubber worn over a man's penis to trap sperm. Condoms that fit into a woman's vagina, work the same way. Women also use *diaphragms,* or cervical caps, and other contraceptive devices to deter sperm by blocking the entrance to a woman's uterus.

The *rhythm method* is a type of birth control that does not require

FAMILY PLANNING—A BASIS NATIONAL POLICY OF CHINA

any equipment. Instead it calls for couples to avoid sexual intercourse during the few days each month when the woman's egg can be fertilized. It is not always easy to predict this brief period accurately, so the rhythm method is considered less reliable than many other contraceptive methods.

For many years it was illegal to sell contraceptives or to supply information about birth control. Attitudes changed in the mid-1900s. Now doctors, pharmacists and groups such as the Planned Parenthood Federation of America provide birth control advice and counseling.

Abortion is not a means of preventing conception, but rather the surgical removal of a fetus from the uterus. Abortion ends a pregnancy, and it remains an issue that divides many people. Supporters of the *Pro-life* movement believe it is wrong. *Pro-choice* supporters argue that the decision to have an abortion should be a private decision made by a woman, and not controlled by law.

Abortion was banned for many years in most states. In 1973, the U.S. Supreme Court made such bans illegal. In a case known as *Roe* v. *Wade* the Court ruled that such state bans infringed a woman's *constitutional* right to privacy. This judgment ensures that a woman's choice to have an abortion early in her pregnancy should be a private decision between herself and her doctor.

Birth control information is becoming widely available in countries with large populations, such as China and India. In such countries, birth control programs are trying to eliminate overcrowding and poverty.

▶▶▶▶ **FIND OUT MORE** ◀◀◀◀
Reproduction

BIRTHDAY

SEE ANNIVERSARY

BIRTHSTONE

SEE GEM

BISMARCK, OTTO VON (1815–1898)

The man who united many small kingdoms into modern, powerful Germany was Otto von Bismarck. He was born in Prussia, now part of northern Germany. Bismarck studied law at the universities of Gottingen and Berlin. After serving in the Prussian legislature for 11 years, he became an ambassador, first to Russia, then to France.

In 1862, he became prime minister of Prussia. Prussia was then one of 39 weak German states. Bismarck wanted to unite all the states into one strong nation. He organized 22 states into the North German Confederation, in 1867, with Prussia as leader.

To unite the rest of Germany, Bismarck steered Prussia into three wars. First, Prussia fought with Austria against Denmark. Then Prussia turned against and defeated Austria. Prussia's war with France, from 1870 to 1871, established the German Empire. The German states not in the confederation helped Prussia win, then found themselves part of the empire.

Wilhelm I became emperor. But Bismarck became *chancellor* (chief minister of state). He ruled for 19 years and made Germany a strong industrial power. He was called the "Iron Chancellor" because he allowed no one to disagree with him. He said that only "iron and blood" could unite Germany. In 1888, Wilhelm II became emperor. He was jealous of Bismarck's power, which he wanted for himself. So he forced Bismarck to retire in 1890.

▶▶▶▶ **FIND OUT MORE** ◀◀◀◀
German History; Germany;
World War I

▲ Otto von Bismarck, German statesman.

▼ The French defeat at the battle of Sedan signaled the end to the Franco-Prussian War (1870–1871). The French were overwhelmed by Prussia's superior forces. Bismarck used the war to bring about the formation of the German Empire.

▲ Bison once roamed the western prairies in vast herds. After being brought close to extinction by hunters, the bison now survives in the safety of game reserves.

▼ Bison have quick tempers, so it has been impossible to tame them. During the breeding season bulls may duel to ward off rivals.

BISON

When people began to explore the American West, they marveled at the large, shaggy brown animals they saw running in great herds. These animals were *bison*, often called the American buffalo.

The bison is a hoofed animal with a humped back and long, coarse hair. The male bison, or bull, ranks as the biggest mammal in North America. It may be 10 feet (3 m) long and as much as 6 feet (1.8 m) tall at the shoulder. The female, or cow, is smaller with a lighter brown coat. Both sexes have small, short horns that curve inward.

The start of the mating season is announced in late summer by loud bellowings, as bulls fight to choose their mates. A single calf is born to each mother the next spring. In a few days the young can run with the herd to search for grass.

Native Americans once hunted bison for their meat, hides, horns, hoofs, and *sinews* (tendons). White settlers and hunters then discovered the valuable animals. Fewer than 600 bison were left by 1899, because thousands were slaughtered to drive out the Native Americans and to clear the land for raising cattle. Laws were passed to protect the remaining animals and slowly the herds became larger. Between 30,000 and 35,000 bison now live in protected areas in both the United States and Canada.

▶ ▶ ▶ ▶ **FIND OUT MORE** ◀ ◀ ◀ ◀
Buffalo; Cattle; Hoofed Animals;
Mammal

BLACK AMERICANS (African Americans)

Did you know that one in every eight citizens has ancestors who came from Africa? Most black Americans are descended from slaves brought against their will to North America in the 17th, 18th, and 19th centuries. Their original homelands were in West Africa. Until the 1960s, the term *Negroes*, which comes from the Spanish word for "black," was used to describe black Americans, as well as blacks in Africa. Today, most black Americans prefer to be called *blacks*, or African-Americans.

African Ancestry

What sort of land did the ancestors of black Americans live in? Some of the greatest African civilizations grew up in West Africa. The empires of Ghana, Mali, and Songhai were rich and powerful. They had very strong armies and well-organized governments.

From the 4th to the 11th century ancient Ghana (which was then much further north than the present country with that name is now) was the most important empire in West Africa. To the north was the Sahara Desert and many of the trade routes across it ended in Ghana. The empire grew rich on trade with Arabs who crossed the Sahara to buy gold and salt.

By 1240, the empire of Mali had overtaken Ghana. Mali reached its peak under Mansa Musa in the early 14th century. Arabs who traveled to the king's court were very impressed by the luxury and wealth they found there. They also found magnificent cities full of palaces and *mosques* (temples). Mali's most famous city, Timbuktu, was the center of Muslim culture and learning.

By the time European explorers arrived in the 15th century, the empire of Songhai dominated West Africa. Arab visitors to the court

noted that there were "many plates and scepters of gold" and that books were sold for more money than any other merchandise.

These empires, and other smaller ones, contributed to the languages, customs, traditions, and arts and crafts of Africa. But many Africans were forced to live another kind of life.

In the 1400s, Portuguese explorers arrived on the African continent. They took black Africans back to Europe as servants. When Christopher Columbus reached America, blacks were with him. Pecho Alonso Niño, one of Columbus's sailors, is believed to have been black. Other black people traveled and worked with the Spanish explorers in South and Central America. Estevanico ("Little Steven") explored northern Mexico and much of what is now Arizona and New Mexico.

When French priests explored Canada, black people were with them, too. Blacks helped build the trading posts that became the cities of St. Louis, Missouri, and New Orleans, Louisiana. Another black, Jean DuSable, built a trading post in 1779. The city of Chicago now stands there.

Slavery in America

Slavery is at least as old as written history. Slaves were usually prisoners taken in war. Sometimes they were criminals. They were forced to do the hard work of pulling the oars in ships, of mining, or farming. But in the Ancient World, slaves were usually permitted to marry, to own property, and even to buy their freedom.

When the New World was discovered, Europeans dreamed of great wealth and power. To make their dreams real, white people needed cheap labor. They soon thought of black Africans, because they could survive in a hot climate, were primitive people, and also different from whites. Blacks looked different, spoke different languages, and were not Christians. These differences made it easier for Europeans to pretend that Africans could not rule themselves, and that it was right for the white people to take over.

The first black slaves arrived in the Spanish colonies of South America in 1501. But they could still buy their freedom, and if they became Christians, they were set free.

In the English colonies of North America, heavy work was done not by slaves, but by *indentured servants*. These people agreed to work for a certain number of years (usually seven or ten) in return for a free trip to America. At the end of that time, the servants became free.

The first indentured servants were English people. Then, in 1619, the first black servants were brought to Jamestown, Virginia. These people were treated just as any other indentured servants. But this changed quickly. The planters in the colonies always had trouble finding workers.

◀ The empires of West Africa not only waged war to win more land but also to win slaves. Captured enemies were marched off to the slave markets on the coast, where they were examined and branded to show they were fit to survive the voyage to America.

There are more than 28 million black American citizens. Two and a half million of them live in New York State.

◀ Mansa Musa, King of Mali, ruled from 1312 to 1337. He is shown here as depicted on a Spanish atlas of 1375.

▼ Africans were brought to North America to work as slaves on Southern plantations. By the early 1800s, about 700,000 slaves lived in the South.

▲ **A Union infantry corporal poses with his pocket revolver during the Civil War.**

▼ **Freed slaves in the North working in a dockyard during the Civil War. It was hoped that the freedom of northern blacks would encourage southern slaves to rebel.**

Colonists tried using Native Americans as workers, but they disappeared into the forests. White indentured servants could easily run away to another colony, where no one would know that they had been servants. When the white servants completed their period of labor, the planters had to find new workers.

Colonists soon realized two things: Blacks could not run away because their black skin color could not be hidden, and they were not Christians. So planters soon began to demand laws that would make slaves of black servants. Virginia passed such a law in 1669. The law stated that black servants were slaves for life, and so were their children. Another law said that even if a black became a Christian, he or she would still be a slave. By 1749, all 13 colonies had similar laws. Black people were no longer individuals, but were pieces of property like a chair or table. There were even laws that said masters could not be accused of murdering their slaves—people would not destroy their own property on purpose!

Southern colonists discovered that three crops—rice, tobacco, and cotton—grew well on their land. All three of these crops required a great deal of land and many workers. The plantations demanded more slaves.

The colonists tried to believe that

black people were contented with their lives as slaves. But the lives of the slaves were usually terrible. They had good food and clothing only if their masters gave them these things. They were not allowed to learn to read or write. Slaves could be beaten. They could be sold, never to see their families again. Slaves could even be killed at the whim of their masters.

The law gave blacks no rights, so they did the only things they could— they fought or they tried to escape. Africans attacked the crews of the ships that carried them to America. Many captives refused to eat and starved themselves to death. Many others drowned themselves. Once in America, many blacks fought against the bonds of slavery. Slaves revolted against their owners. About two hundred slave revolts occurred in the United States alone.

But blacks were sometimes expected to fight with the whites, not against them. Blacks fought in the Revolutionary War (and in every American war since). Black soldiers of the Revolution include: Deborah Gannett, who, disguised as a man, fought the British for 18 months, winning a medal for her heroism; Salem Poor, who fought in the battle of Bunker Hill in Boston; Peter Salem, who killed the British commander at the Battle of Bunker Hill; and Crispus Attucks, who was killed earlier during the Boston Massacre. But when the Revolutionary War

was over, these brave soldiers were quickly forgotten by some. Black Americans were thought of only as slaves in the new Southern states. But the Northern states thought differently. Vermont outlawed slavery in 1777, and by 1804, all the Northern states had abolished it.

By the time the Civil War broke out 15 of the states had slaves, and 18 had no slavery. The Civil War produced many black heroes and heroines. For example, before the fighting began, Harriet Tubman escaped from slavery in the South and returned many times to lead more than 300 other slaves to freedom. She also worked as a nurse for the Union Army.

After the Civil War ended in 1865, the Thirteenth Amendment to the Constitution was passed, and slavery was declared illegal in the United States. For the first time, blacks were regarded as a free people by the Constitution. But the fight for equality was far from over.

Picking Up the Pieces

The South was in ruins at the end of the Civil War. Fields were covered with weeds, houses were wrecked, families were separated. The freed blacks had no jobs and no money. They did not trust the whites and the whites did not trust them.

Southern whites soon took control of state governments. They passed local laws meant to keep blacks from being treated as their equals. Black people were not allowed to travel freely or to testify in court against white people. Other laws stated that blacks without jobs would be fined. Those who could not pay the fine would be forced to work for someone who would pay it. Many blacks were effectively made slaves again.

Congress passed a law giving the Union Army control of the Southern state governments, and most of the unfair Southern laws were overturned. This was the period known

as *Reconstruction* (rebuilding), which lasted from 1865 to 1877. During this time, many blacks were elected to public office. Robert Smalls, who captured the Confederate ship *Planter* and later commanded it for the Union, was elected to Congress, as was Francis Cardozo. Blanche Bruce served in the U.S. Senate, as did Hiram R. Revels. Pinckney B. S. Pinchback became governor of Louisiana and was elected to the U.S. Senate in 1873. White senators said he was not "cooperative," and

they refused to let him take his place. Many other blacks served in state legislatures.

But many Southern whites opposed growing black power and criticized the North. By the early 1870s, the North had grown tired of spending time and money on the South. Union troops were gradually withdrawn and black leaders were voted out of office, one by one. By 1877, all Union troops were gone from the South, whites controlled the governments, and Reconstruction was finished.

Black Leaders

When Reconstruction was over, Southern governments again passed laws that practically made black people slaves. Blacks had to ride in separate railroad cars, use separate drinking fountains, and attend separate schools. They were restricted from voting by various laws, and secret societies, such as the Ku Klux

▲ Three heroes of American history: Frederick Douglass (center) fearlessly campaigned against slavery in the 1840s; in 1870, Hiram R. Revels (right), a Republican became the first black senator; and Blanche Bruce (left) was the first black to serve a full six-year term in the Senate.

From the year 1808, no slaves could be brought into the United States. But in 1860, there were still almost 4 million black slaves working in the country, nearly one-third of the total population of the Southern states.

▲ Members of the Ku Klux Klan at a rally in 1923. Founded in 1866 to oppose the advancement of blacks, the Klan, though suppressed, has reappeared several times, especially in the 1960s.

▼ In 1991, Colin Powell, then head of the Joint Chiefs of Staff, helped plan the defeat of Iraq in the Persian Gulf War.

▶ Patricia Roberts Harris was ambassador to Luxembourg before serving as Secretary of Housing and Urban Development from 1977 to 1979 under President Jimmy Carter.

Klan, terrorized blacks and discouraged them from exercising their rights.

By the early 1900s, new black leaders began to emerge. One leader was Booker T. Washington. He believed that black people needed training before they could construct buildings, manage factories, and grow crops. He was afraid that blacks would move too quickly in making the change from slavery to freedom, bringing about more problems than successes. Many blacks supported Washington's ideas, as did many whites.

Other black leaders disagreed with Washington. One of the most important was W.E.B. Du Bois, who was born in Massachusetts, the son of a successful lawyer. Du Bois said blacks were not moving fast enough. He demanded immediate full and equal rights for all blacks.

In 1909, Du Bois and many other black leaders joined with a group of white people to form the National Association for the Advancement of Colored People (NAACP). This organization has won many legal battles that have helped to defend the rights black people were guaranteed in the Thirteenth Amendment.

Two other black groups were formed at about the same time. The Urban League's purpose was to help black people adjust to living in large northern cities. The Universal Negro Improvement Association was led by Marcus Garvey. Garvey was the first person to use the saying, "Black Is Beautiful."

The Start of Civil Rights

The Depression of the 1930s brought hard times for blacks and whites, but blacks suffered more. They used the slogan "Last Hired and First Fired" to express their bitterness about the unfair treatment they received.

The end of World War II in 1945 brought the start of the civil rights movement. Many blacks had served with honor in the war, while at home blacks had benefited from increased opportunities in work and education. Working through the courts, many laws allowing racial discrimination were overturned. In one legal case in 1954, the Supreme Court said that segregated schools (separate schools for black children and white children) were illegal because "separate" cannot be "equal."

Other organizations, such as the Southern Christian Leadership Conference (once led by Martin Luther King Jr.), used marches and nonviolent demonstrations to bring about change. Some groups, such as the Black Muslims, thought white prejudice would never change. They stressed independence for blacks and established separate, black-owned businesses, stores, farms, and schools.

Blacks Today

Blacks have had to fight for rights that whites of European ancestry have been able to take for granted from birth. They have gained many of those rights, particularly in the years since the 1960s.

Black people have entered many occupations that were once closed to them. Colleges and universities admit

blacks and often provide scholar-ships for those who cannot afford tuition. The numbers of blacks in such institutions has increased by more than 50 percent since 1970.

Blacks now hold professional jobs, run their own businesses, and serve in elective offices. Thurgood Marshall became the first black Associate Justice of the U.S. Supreme Court in 1967. Patricia Roberts Harris became the first black woman in the Cabinet when President Jimmy Carter appointed her Secretary of Housing and Urban Development. In 1989, Douglas Wilder was elected governor of Virginia, becoming the nation's first black governor since the 1870s. In the same year Colin Powell became chairman of the Joint Chiefs of Staff, the highest post in the U.S. military. In 1992, Carol Moseley-Braun became the first black woman senator.

But prejudice against blacks still exists. The unemployment rate for blacks is more than double the rate for whites. Many black leaders believe this can only be solved by political means. David Dinkins was the first black mayor of New York City. Although he is no longer mayor, the number of black mayors throughout the country continues to grow. In the 1984 and 1988 presidential campaigns, the Rev. Jesse Jackson, a Baptist minister, made a strong bid to run as the Democratic candidate. Jackson had already made a name for himself as a civil rights leader and founder of Operation PUSH (People United to Serve Humanity). It is one of many organizations through which blacks are still fighting for complete equality with whites.

Black leaders, writers, and artists are urging blacks to be proud of their African and American ancestry. Today, blacks know what they are legally entitled to as citizens.

▶ ▶ ▶ ▶ **FIND OUT MORE** ◀ ◀ ◀ ◀
Black People in the Arts see
Anderson, Marian; Armstrong, Louis; Baldwin, James; Brooks, Gwendolyn; Handy, W.C.; Hughes, James Langston; Jackson, Mahalia; Wright, Richard
Black People in Government see
Brooke, Edward; Bruce, Blanche K.; Bunche, Ralph; Chisolm, Shirley; Harris, Patricia Roberts; Jackson, Jesse; Marshall, Thurgood; Young, Andrew
Black People in Science see
Carver, George Washington; Burbank, Luther
Black People in Sports see Ali, Muhammad; Gibson, Althea; Owens, Jesse; Robinson, Jackie
Black People in Education see
Bethune, Mary McLeod; Washington, Booker T.
Early Black History see Africa; Estevanico; Slavery
Black History in the Eighteenth Century see American Colonies; Banneker, Benjamin; Revolutionary War
Black History in the Nineteenth Century see Abolition; Civil War; Confederate States of America; Douglass, Frederick; Emancipation Proclamation; Reconstruction; Truth, Sojourner; Tubman, Harriet;

▲ The novelist Alice Walker who won the 1983 Pulitzer Prize for fiction for her novel *The Color Purple*. The novel tells the story of two sisters who lived in the cruel, segregated world of the Deep South between the two World Wars.

▼ Florence Griffith Joyner proudly shows the medals she won in the 1988 Olympic games at Seoul. She won gold medals in the 100-meter run, the 200-meter run, and the 400-meter relay.

◀ Spike Lee, the much acclaimed actor and film director. His films often look at the problems many blacks face living in a white society.

Turner, Nat; Underground Railroad; Washington, Booker T.
Black History in the Twentieth Century see Civil Rights; Civil Rights Movement; Davis Family; King, Martin Luther, Jr.; Malcolm X; National Association for the Advancement of Colored People; Young, Whitney Moore

◀ **A Blackfoot Indian wearing the traditional skin shirt and leggings of his people. In the winter a bison robe was also wrapped around the shoulders to keep out the terrible cold.**

BLACKFOOT

The Blackfoot Confederacy was a group of three tribes who lived in the area where Montana and the Canadian Provinces of Saskatchewan and Alberta lie today. The tribes were the Siksika (Blackfoot proper), the Piegan, and the Blood. They were often talked about as one group and called the Blackfeet. They roamed the plains, following the bison (American buffalo) herds. The bison was vital to the life of the Blackfeet. They ate bison meat and made colorful tepees from the hides. They also made warm robes, cooking vessels, saddles, and moccasins. They dyed their moccasins black, which may have given the tribe its name.

The Blackfeet spoke an Algonkian (Algonquian) language. They hunted in various ways. Some Blackfeet would drive a herd of bison over a cliff to get meat and hides for all.

When Spanish explorers brought horses to America, the Blackfeet learned to hunt bison on horseback. But in the 19th century, the bison disappeared from the plains and so did the Blackfoot way of life. Today they live as farmers and ranchers. They live on a reservation in Montana, and on three Canadian reserves.

▶▶▶▶ **FIND OUT MORE** ◀◀◀◀
Algonkian; Native Americans

QUIZ ANSWERS

Asia quiz, page 264
1. The Gobi desert lies in northern China and southern Mongolia.
2. Monsoons are strong winds. In the summer they accompany fierce rain; in winter they blow dry and dusty.
3. The orangutan is native to southeast Asia, notably Borneo and Sumatra.
4. The smallest nation in size is Macao, a peninsula and two small islands located at the mouth of the Canton River in China. It measures 6 square miles (16 km²).
5. The smallest nation in population are the Maldive Islands, southwest of India, with 200,000 citizens.
6. Most of the Tibetan people practice Buddhism. Tibet is now a region of China, but it was once part of India.
7. The Chinese belong to the Mongoloid group; the Iranians to the Caucasoid group.

Australia quiz, page 289
1. The temperature gets cooler the further south you go. This is because Australia is in the southern hemisphere, so the further north you go the closer you are to the equator (where temperatures are very hot), while the further south you go, the closer you are to the South Pole (Antarctica).
2. *Aborigine* comes from the word "aboriginal," which means a person or thing that is the first of its kind. The white settlers called the people they found living in Australia aborigines since these people had obviously been the country's first inhabitants.
3. The largest city in Australia is Sydney, with 3,531,000 people.
4. Wool, beef, leather, dairy products, wheat, cereals, sugar, and fruit are all major exports.
5. Yes, koalas are marsupials.

Bicycle quiz, page 363
1. A *unicycle* has just one wheel; a *tricycle* has three.
2. The first bicycle was built in Europe in about 1690.
3. The Tour de France is held every year in summer, usually in July.
4. You reverse the pedals quickly, causing the wheels to stop rotating and making the bike stop.

Bird quiz, page 369
1. Alaska's state bird is the willow ptarmigan, a variety of grouse that favors the northern climate. Vermont's is the hermit thrush.
2. Over 800 species of birds make their homes in North America.
3. Yes, all birds have feathers, but they can't all fly: ostriches can't fly, neither can penguins, although penguins can swim.
4. The ostrich is the largest bird in the world.